TABLE
DECORATIONS

TABLE DECORATIONS

AUDREY ELLIS

WARD LOCK

© Audrey Ellis 1978, 1989
Illustrations © Ward Lock 1989

This revised edition by Jane Pettigrew
first published in Great Britain in 1989
by Ward Lock, Villiers House, 41/47 Strand, London WC2N 5JE

First paperback edition 1990

A Cassell imprint.

Text filmset in Bauer Bodoni
by Facet Film Composing Ltd, Leigh-on-Sea, Essex

Printed and bound in Spain by Graficas Reunidas

British Library Cataloguing in Publication Data
Ellis, Audrey
    Table decorations.
        1.   Tables. Decoration–Manuals
        1.   Title
        642′.8

ISBN 0–7063–6915–7

CONTENTS

INTRODUCTION

A beautiful and appropriate table layout sets the scene for an enjoyable meal and, with a little know-how and lots of imagination, attractive colour schemes and toning flower arrangements can be created for any occasion from an informal lunch to an elegant formal dinner.

Few households possess more than one set of china, glassware and cutlery, so it is important to be able to work around these items, creating different moods and effects with linens, flowers, candles and lighting. These should be planned for each particular occasion and for each specific menu so that the food and drink are enhanced by their setting.

This book is designed to give basic information on choosing and buying furniture, china, serving pieces, cutlery and other accessories, and on how to look after them, as well as offering ideas on mixing and matching tableware to create those different settings.

An elegant celebration buffet for a special family occasion

1 ESSENTIAL FURNITURE

When you shop for dining-room furniture and table accessories it pays to have a general plan in mind for the kind of life you lead, both in terms of daily eating and entertaining friends.

THE RIGHT TABLE

Your dining-table need not be a valuable antique or masterpiece of modern design. It could come from an auction, junk shop or modern sales department. What is important is that it is the right height with space to give enough elbow room for people to sit comfortably around it. The shape is important, as is the size and placing of the legs, because these considerations affect the way it can be set, and how many people can be accommodated. Have in mind the number who will usually be present at mealtimes and the largest number you might reasonably wish to seat for special occasions. Can you manage with a table which will not extend, or must it be adaptable with gatelegs or extra leaves to be fitted when required? Should a table be large enough for buffet parties? These are some of the questions you should ask yourself when searching for the ideal table.

Size and shape

Whether choosing antique or modern furniture, decide calmly and not on impulse. Furniture always looks smaller in the shop than it does at home so have a plan of your room on squared paper, one square equalling 1 m (3 ft), with you when shopping. Measure the table and sketch it on your plan to show how much space it will occupy. Consider, too, the size and shape of your dining-room or dining area. Massive furniture tends to overwhelm a small room and delicate ornamental pieces look insignificant in a large one. Ideally each person needs 60 cm (24 in) of table edge; 75 cm (29 in) of table depth and 25-30 cm (10-12 in) between the chair seat and the table top.

Room Mates

A dining-room or dining area should never look overcrowded.

A round table might best suit a small square room, because of the contrast in shape. The table itself need not be very large. Chairs can be placed fairly close together to seat guests. Some round tables can become ovals if fitted with a central leaf.

An oval table will suit almost any shape of room, and the table can probably be extended to become an elongated oval by adding a leaf. Again, shape contrast is given to a room which is not completely square by introducing pleasantly curved lines.

An oblong table like the reproduction Jacobean refectory table, looks well in a room large enough to give plenty of space between the chairs and the walls; otherwise the impression is of an oblong within an oblong which produces an unattractive geometric pattern.

Where space is limited and the number you can seat is all-important, remember that tables change shape when leaves are inserted or gateleg-supported flaps raised. Check how the supports stand because the position of extra legs on the latter type of table can make seating cramped. The refectory table provides a maximum surface area for a minimum of legs (usually one central support running the entire length or simply a leg at each corner). Generally speaking, look for a table which does not exactly echo the shape of the room.

When buying old tables be aware of damage to the surface. Table mats and cloths can be used to hide damage but, if the purpose of buying an antique or old table is to have the attractive wood on show, scratches and grooves or damaged veneer or French polishing will have to be repaired. Scratches and grooves can be filled and stained but they will not be completely concealed. Professional restoration can work miracles but is very expensive, so do think carefully.

When choosing modern designs, shop around, scan magazines and send off for catalogues before buying. Unless you are an expert go to a reputable dealer. Most modern tables seat four normally and eight at the most. Can the table be extended? Is the design functional, and in a style you can live with for many years, or will it date? Find out exactly what it is made of. Is it solid wood, or veneer and chipboard, or laminate? You can tell solid wood, which, incidentally, might also be veneered with a more expensive wood, by looking for grain-end at the table edge. Check the workmanship; look underneath for bad joints, rough finishing, loose screws, blobs of glue, and finally, the overall finish. Find out from the manufacturer how best to care for the table, whether it will withstand heat from hot dishes or from radiators or open or gas fires. (New wood often takes less kindly to temperature changes than old.)

Making do
Special occasions that overstretch your normal seating and table space only happen a few times a year in most households. If you have to supplement your non-extendable four-seater with a card table at one end, make a larger fit-on top to go over the dining-table. Use 19 mm (¾ in) chipboard — the supplier will cut it into shape. Clip it securely to the existing table with wooden swivel clips and add extra slip-in legs made from 25 mm (1 in) dowelling to either side for added stability. Remember to cover your own table first with a protective cloth to prevent scratching.

CHAIRS
Your dining-table naturally governs the style of chair you choose to go with it. The chairs may come with the table as a matching set in which case the problem is solved. Or is it? It is not very satisfactory to buy a table which seems perfect at the time unless the chairs that go with it are comfortable and suit the dining space. If the dining area is part of an open-plan living-room, make sure that the upright chairs tone with the armchairs and sofa.

How many chairs?
The size of the table, fully extended if it has leaves, will determine how many chairs will fit comfortably around it. Chairs that are too wide or uncomfort-

ably narrow are impractical. A seat of about 90 cm (35 in) square is a good average size. The height of the seat must also suit the height of the table and leave plenty of leg room.

A basic set of chairs is usually four or six, but you may need more later. When you buy, check with the supplier whether the style and pattern are likely to be repeatable so that chairs may be bought individually at a later date. If there is any doubt that this will be possible, buy the chairs all at once and tuck the spares into bedrooms or the hallway if the dining-room is too small to take them all.

Choose for comfort

Make sure that your new chairs really are built strongly enough for people to sit on, and that they don't groan or rock precariously. If choosing antique or second-hand chairs, remember that it can be expensive to have joints repaired or seating replaced. A good test is to sit on a chair, rocking it on to the back legs; ominous creaks are a sure sign that it may not wear well. To test for comfort, sit on one of the chairs for several minutes, preferably pulled up to a table. Is it comfortable – does it support the back – do your legs fit under the table comfortably?

Do you want arm rests? Dining-chairs with arms are called 'carvers' and are usually placed at each end of the table. They are not really practical with a round table.

LIGHTING

The right kind of lighting can make or mar the look of a table, but many novel and ingenious effects are possible with electric lights and/or candles. Do you intend to place a centre light over the table? Or do you plan to have wall-sconces and no centre light? A fitting which can be raised or lowered over the table centre is much the most convenient, and can be fixed for most occasions at the height at which it conveys most harmony to the shape of the room and gives the best light; usually about 75 cm (30 in) above the table. Choose a shade that sheds a diffused light, as direct lighting can be too harsh. You may like to fit an electric dimmer switch on the wall, to give more or less light to suit the occasion. Big lamps on the sideboard give an angled light and this is not very practical because the diners will sit between it and the food, casting shadows over the table. Some direct lighting on or over the table is therefore essential.

2   TABLE LINENS

TABLE-CLOTHS

Traditionally the cloth laid over the table for a dinner-party was white and a lot of people still prefer the crisp clean look of spotless white linen or cotton, but coloured cloths play such an important part in creating different moods and effects that it is a matter of personal choice as to which is best for a particular occasion.

Choosing table-cloths

The size is the most important thing to bear in mind. Ideally, whether square or round, the cloth should hang about half-way down to the floor. When shopping for cloths do have a note of your table measurements with you.

You also need to consider the material the cloth is made from and ask yourself how often you will have to wash and iron it. For very special occasions, damask linens and embroidered linens look the most attractive, but they do take far more care than cotton or polyester. You may not mind laundering something as difficult as linen just once in a while, whereas a table-cloth for everyday use needs to be very easy to care for. Cotton seersucker is probably the easiest, and most cottons and poly-cottons wash well and are easy to iron or need no ironing. For a kitchen table made of a wood that marks easily, a bright plastic-coated cloth is an excellent choice at mealtimes. These vinyl coverings are readily available and can be cut to any size. They are generally heat resistant, add colour to the kitchen and are very easy to wipe clean.

Making your own table-cloths

If you enjoy sewing and embroidering, it is much cheaper to make your own cloths and matching napkins. Good department stores often sell Terylene-cotton or polyester-cotton sheeting with simple stylized motifs in various colours on a white background. They may also stock the same fabric with the motif reduced to half size. This means you can make a cloth in the larger pattern and napkins in the scaled down motif. Mail order firms also sell polyester and cotton easy-care sheeting in strong or pastel shades so there is a wide choice and flexibility. Table-cloths can also be matched to or co-ordinated with the curtains in the dining-room.

Protecting your table-top

Even with heat-resistant mats placed on top of the cloth there is always the risk of wood being damaged by hot dishes and stains through the cloth. It is a good idea to make a heat-resistant cover that fits the table-top exactly and then to lay the cloth over this. The thinnest and least conspicuous material for this purpose is Bulgomme which is made of rubber. It has a surface that looks rather like linen and although it is only about 5 mm (¼ in) thick it gives as good protection as the average heat-resistant mat. An alternative to this is a covering of green baize or felt, cut so that it just covers the table and does not show below the edge of the table-cloth.

NAPKINS

For formal occasions linen napkins are best and should match or tone with the table-cloth or mats. For informal meals and snacks, paper napkins are perfectly acceptable and come in such a wide range of colours and designs that you should be able to match any colour cloth or china.

The way you arrange or fold napkins depends largely on whether they match or contrast with the cloth, and also on the size. In the days when napkins were large and made to match the cloth, the material could be folded into fancy shapes to create exciting and attractive designs. Today, napkins tend to be smaller and of a different colour or pattern and so an interesting effect is most easily achieved with a few simple folds.

Folding napkins decoratively

To create an exciting design a large napkin, preferably starched, and at least 40 cm (15 in) square is needed. It must be absolutely square and even all over. When buying napkins, unfold them and check this carefully.

If using napkins that are about 35 cm (13 in) square, or less, the simplest ways to present them are as follows:

1 Fold the napkin in four to make a smaller square and then across diagonally to make a triangle.

2 Fold the napkin in half and then three times, concertina fashion.

3 Roll loosely and secure with a decorative napkin ring.

4 Use a simple napkin ring decorated with fresh flowers or furled toning satin ribbons.

1 *Candle*

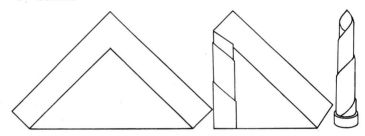

2 *Fan*

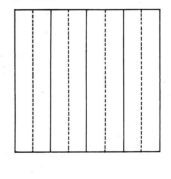

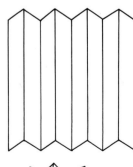

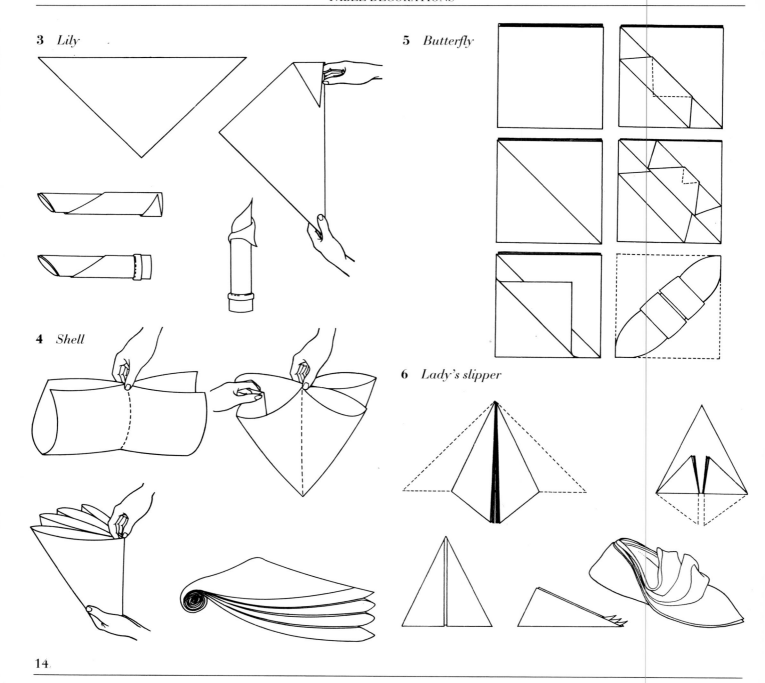

3 *Lily*

4 *Shell*

5 *Butterfly*

6 *Lady's slipper*

7 *Mitre*

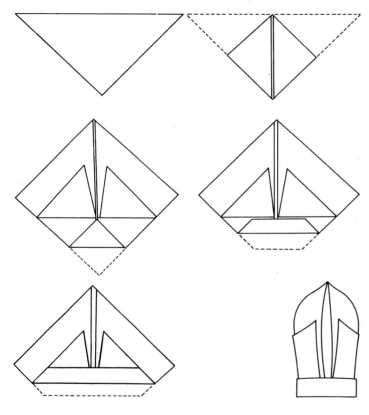

8 *Heart*

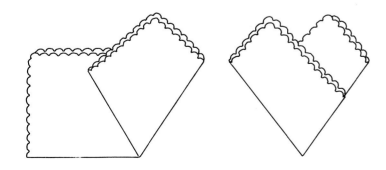

9 *Clown's hat*

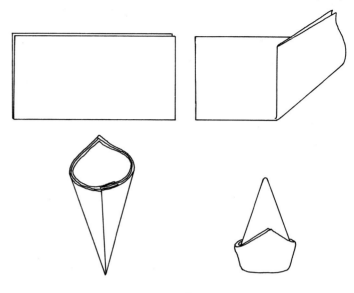

TABLE-MATS

If you wish to show off a beautiful wooden table-top and set the table without a cloth, it is essential to protect the surface from heat and stains by using mats. The best mats are heat-proof and cork backed, with laminated or melamine surfaces, and need only a wipe with a damp cloth to clean them. They come in many designs, usually with coasters and serving mats as well as place mats to match.

Heat-proof and damp-proof mats

Good quality mats are sometimes labelled showing exactly what degree of heat they will resist. This should be at least 60°C (140°F). Very hot casseroles

White damask or lace napkins are all that are needed to complete this setting for a formal dinner

may do untold damage through a thin mat, so it is best to use a cork mat or other heat-resistant material underneath. If in doubt, place one mat on top of another. Be very careful if you are using padded cloth mats under hot dishes, because these will also need a cork mat underneath them.

If your mats have a thin lining of baize stuck underneath them, take care never to get the underside of the mat wet. Always clean mats after use to keep them free from grease and marks.

Washable mats
Antique markets and shops often have old-fashioned lace and embroidered covers for cork mats which are extremely attractive. These mats often come in sets for cocktail glasses, coasters, place settings and serving mats. They do, however, need very careful laundering and sometimes starching. Modern washable mats are often more easily laundered but they do need frequent washing to keep them fresh and free from stains.

3 CHINA, GLASSWARE AND CUTLERY

CHINA

The term 'china' is used to describe widely different materials ranging from the finest porcelain to heavy earthenware pottery. Fine china is usually kept for entertaining and a heavier duty pottery or earthenware is used every day.

Porcelain and bone china

This is the very best china and, treated carefully, will last well. Its extremely delicate appearance is deceptive, for it is remarkably robust and, unless knocked quite hard, is far more resistant to chipping than one might expect. It should not, however, be put into or on a very hot oven but should be warmed very gently. Overheating will cause tiny cracks to appear in the glaze and the lustre will disappear. Fine china should never come into contact with direct heat such as a low gas flame.

China decorated with gold or silver leaf is very expensive and needs very careful treatment. Constant washing in a dish washer will easily damage the metal decoration, and although a gentle scour is often needed to remove tannin stains from the inside of the cup, such rough treatment is not suitable for the outer part.

China with any form of metallic finish should never be put inside a microwave oven. It will ruin both the china and the oven.

Pottery (earthenware and stoneware)

The price range in this category is quite wide as unglazed earthenware dishes are understandably cheaper than oven-proof stoneware. Unglazed pottery is porous, dries out unless pre-soaked when exposed to extreme heat in the conventional oven, and is liable to crack. Glazed earthenware is more durable but the most hard-wearing type is stoneware, equally suitable for use in the oven and for serving food on the table. All these types can safely be used for microwave cooking.

Some earthenware has a decorative pattern applied before the glaze is put on and at first glance might be mistaken for china.

CHOOSING YOUR CHINA

When choosing your china you must decide whether you wish to collect a particular design for breakfast, dinner and tea services, or whether each set is to be different; in which case what will happen when the set becomes depleted by breakages?

If you are starting to collect a service of china, make certain you choose a pattern that can be repeated when you want or can afford to buy more.

One reasonably inexpensive way to acquire good china is to buy 'seconds'. These are frequently offered at sale time or may be purchased from the manufacturer's factory shop. If you do buy 'seconds', which usually sell for about a third of the price of perfect goods, it is better to choose pieces with pattern flaws rather than misshapen pieces. The pattern flaws are usually very hard to detect so friends and family who use them will not realize they are not perfect.

It is not always necessary to buy new china to acquire full dinner or tea sets. Junk shops, antique shops, markets and auctions often have the most beautiful period pieces, sometimes in full sets, sometimes in part sets. For anyone who loves collecting it is a real challenge, and great fun, to scour the local area or the country to find more pieces to add to a part set of Victorian china or a beautiful art deco set from the 1920s. Period china can be matched to period furniture and whole table settings made up to recreate a past era, with cruet sets, cutlery, glasses and candlesticks of matching style.

GLASSWARE

Formerly a full suite of glasses would contain anything from ten to twenty different shapes. Nowadays we make do with far fewer and the rules as to their use are less rigid. There are many different qualities and designs available and it is generally possible to find attractive glasses to suit your budget. There are two main kinds to be aware of, lead crystal and soda glass.

Lead crystal is the most expensive hand-made glass and it contains lead oxide. Because of its high light refraction it displays the contents to the finest advantage, and lends itself best to decorative cutting. Within this section there are several grades, so enquire carefully from the retailer the exact description of the high-quality glass to guide you on price. A printed price list should indicate the grades.

The highest quality contains about 30% lead oxide and is distinguished by the name, 'Full Lead Crystal'. The next highest grade is 'Lead Crystal', containing slightly less lead oxide; the third grade is 'Lead Glass'. The higher the lead content the heavier the glass. All such glassware is brilliantly clear, relatively heavy, and will ring with a resonant tone when tapped. This is the table glass you will probably keep for parties only. It can be embellished with various decorations, principally by cutting and engraving. Deep cutting in elaborate patterns produces the most brilliant effect but is, naturally, the most expensive. Intaglio cutting is lighter, and therefore less costly. Beautiful effects are also produced by engraving with a copper wheel or stylus, but the result is more subtle than the bright sparkle of cut glass. The two methods can actually be combined in the same piece.

Soda glass is a more moderately priced glass made from soda ash and silica sand. Nevertheless it can be of very high quality. Soda glass can be hand blown but is more frequently machine-made. It is more often pressed than cut, therefore the edges are not as sharp as lead glass and the light refraction is not as good.

Lead crystal is expensive and it is worth remembering that you may want to add to your set in the future. You are more likely to find that a classic lead crystal is repeatable, whereas modern, fashionable designs are more likely to disappear from the market as tastes in shape and design change. Always ask, when buying, whether the pattern, size and shape will be exactly the same in future batches.

Some glass makers are able to offer the special service of etching a monogram, motif or special design on to your glasses.

Coloured glass

The fine lead crystal glass that we take for granted today has only been generally available for the last 200 years. It reveals the quality and beautiful colour of wine or other drinks, whereas antique coloured glass changes or hides the colour.

Coloured glass can be used to tone with coloured china and to blend or contrast with the colour schemes used for linens and flowers. Antique shops and junk markets often stock old, coloured glass. The warmer colours – amber, tawny pinks and golden yellows – are kinder to the colour of wine than the greens and blues.

CHOOSING GLASSES

For informal meals you need not worry about which shape wine glass to use and for formal occasions the following guidelines can be followed.

The short-stemmed goblet is intended for red wines so that your hand can naturally encircle the glass, so warming it.

Claret glasses are tulip shaped to retain the bouquet.

Burgundies, on the other hand, are best drunk from wider glasses.

White wines should be served chilled in long-stemmed glasses. This is so that the hand only touches the stem and does not warm the wine.

A champagne glass should be a tulip or flute shape to help retain the sparkle.

Sherry and Port

These glasses come in various shapes but should have a smaller capacity than wine glasses. The copita or small tulip shape is most suitable. Glasses for port, madeira or other fortified wines are not as tall as sherry glasses.

10 *Shapes of drinking glasses*

white wine   red wine   champagne

sherry   port   liqueur   cocktail

brandy   highball   whisky

Liqueurs

Liqueur glasses are tiny, as the correct quantity served is small. Many shapes are available, the most usual being like a miniature claret glass. A large liqueur glass can be used for brandy, but a balloon glass is best as it allows the warmth of the hand to warm the glass and release the aroma to fill it.

Other glasses

Whisky is normally drunk from straight sided tumblers. Neat vodka and other spirits are usually served in small, slim conical glasses with no stems. Cocktail glasses are usually of a wider, conical shape with a stem, as cocktails are usually served chilled or with crushed ice. American highball glasses are traditionally tall and straight-sided. Popular 'mixed' drinks, such as gin and tonic, should be served in highball glasses because the tall slim shape helps to conserve the bubbles of the mineral. Beer is served in a large goblet or tankard.

Decanters and carafes

Decanters are usually stoppered to prevent loss of bouquet from fine old red wines. Spirit decanters which often come in pairs may be simple yet elegant in shape, but are more often made of deeply etched glass. These too need stoppers. Silver tags hung round the necks identify the contents.

Robust young red wines benefit from exposure to the oxidizing process of air and are frequently served in a carafe, which has no stopper.

CUTLERY

The price of cutlery varies enormously according to the material it is made from and the quality of the finish. At the lowest end of the scale is stainless steel cutlery, although this rises in price depending on the quality of the steel and the degree of workmanship. Stainless steel is extremely practical and suits informal meals, but it is not always appropriate for more formal occasions.

Next in the price range comes cutlery made of stainless steel with wood, bone, china or stoneware handles. Silver-plated cutlery follows, with the price again dependent on the thickness and quality of the plate and the workmanship involved. Few people today can afford solid silver cutlery, so silver plate, especially Sheffield plate (which is silver-plated copper) is a perfectly acceptable alternative.

Pewter is another option. Modern pewter is much improved on the old variety, containing no lead (which was a health hazard and also caused blackening). The eating parts are generally made of stainless steel and the cutlery can safely be washed in a dish-washer. The handles may be silver-plated or finished simply with the soft subtle glow of pewter. In either case any tarnishing may be removed easily with a good silver polish.

Bronze is also popular for cutlery and is as easy to care for as silver. Top of the price list and outside most people's budget is gold-dipped steel.

Before you make your choice, spare some thought for the time you can afford keeping your cutlery clean. Stainless steel is the easiest and will stand up to constant washing in a dish-washer. Unless badly stained it needs no special cleaning or polishing although you can buy cleaning materials for stainless steel which can be used to brighten dull items. Bone or wood handles do not stand up well to prolonged immersion in water, so need very careful washing to keep the handles out of water. Silver cutlery needs regular cleaning and polishing but there are products available which keep them untarnished for quite a long time.

Size and pattern

Cutlery is made in an enormous range of styles and sizes. The decision on style is, of course, a matter of individual taste and is probably governed by what will match the rest of the tableware you have or hope to acquire. Size has more practical considerations. Hold and feel the cutlery before you decide. Do you find the balance acceptable and do the handles fit comfortably into your palms or rest on your fingers?

Quantities

If you are short of funds then you can cope initially with a knife, fork and spoon apiece. In such circumstances it makes good sense to buy a repeatable pattern and build up your stock gradually. The leading British manufacturers sell cutlery in full canteens for six or twelve or more settings, in individual place settings and some designs in individual pieces. You can also buy special steak knives and forks in sets of six.

A typical place setting comprises the following: meat knife, butter/cheese/dessert knife, meat fork, dessert fork, soup spoon, dessert spoon and teaspoon. If you make a practice of serving starters other than soup, you may need extra cutlery such as small pointed grapefruit spoons. Melon is eaten with a small knife and fork, or a spoon and fork if preferred, and hors d'oeuvres with a small fork only. A set of pearl-handled or unusual cutlery, co-ordinated with, but not matching anything else, may be used for starters. The forks can double at tea-time for eating pastries in place of conventional pastry forks. Many canteens and place settings include teaspoons and coffee spoons, but not all. Proper coffee spoons are smaller because after-dinner coffee is traditionally served in small cups.

Cruet sets

Enclosed salt and pepper pots are designed to take pre-ground salt and pepper. For peppercorns and salt crystals, which actually give a far better flavour, you need pepper and salt mills. These are usually made from wood or perspex and range from 7-10 cm (3-4 in) tall to 30 cm (12 in) tall. The grinding blades will not last forever and cannot be resharpened but good-quality mills will last for a number of years.

For formal occasions old-fashioned salt cellars are very suitable. These are usually made from glass, silver or porcelain and the salt is transferred to the side of the plate with a small silver spoon. Mustard is also served in a small container with a glass liner and spoon.

A wide range of matching cruet sets is generally available, and it is worth hunting for antique or second-hand sets which can be extremely pretty, and tone with antique or second-hand china and glassware to create a period effect.

SPECIAL DISHES

Among the 'special' dishes or sets of dishes you might like to acquire are those for a particular food. The following are the most usual.

Artichoke plates

These round dishes, embossed with a raised design of artichoke leaves, have a circular depression in the centre for the artichoke and a dimple for melted butter or french dressing.

Avocado dishes

These come in exactly the right shape to hold half an avocado, and are made from glass or fine bone china embossed with leaves.

11 *Artichoke dish*

12 *Avocado dish*

13 *Escargot dish*

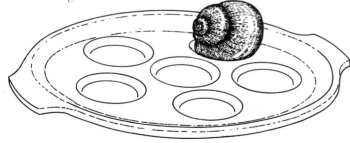

14 *Corn-on-the-cob dish*

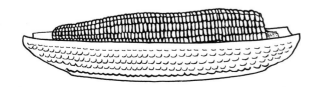

15 *Oyster plate*

Snail plates

These are round metal, china or pottery dishes made with small indentations to hold from six to twelve snails.

Corn-on-the-cob dishes

These are usually made from white china, fashioned in the shape of a leafy cradle in which the cob lies.

Oyster plates

Round bone china dishes with well-shaped indentations to hold six oysters and a small bowl in the middle to hold a sauce.

Serving dishes

It is perfectly acceptable to use stoneware, earthenware or pottery dishes on the table for informal occasions, but for elegant formal dinners it is better to use dishes that match the dinner service or that are finer and prettier than most stoneware or earthenware. Most dinner services include vegetable dishes with matching lids and large oval plates for serving meat; these are also excellent for serving arrangements of different salads or vegetables.

For special dishes such as potted shrimps, pâtés, soufflées or flans, plain white china is available which will blend with almost any style of tableware. A gravy or sauce boat is an important item and often

The novelty cake, brightly-coloured toys and sugar ducks add fun to the farmyard theme for a children's party

available as part of a dinner service. If not, you could buy one in stainless steel, plated silver or china. A matching ladle is useful and generally available, or you could browse in second-hand and antique shops among the collections of different-sized ladles in plated silver or porcelain.

A salad bowl is essential, and the best are made from glass or wood with matching servers. You will also need: a butter dish or plate that is pretty enough to be used on formal occasions; a container such as a delicate basket or pretty china dish for bread rolls, buttered bread or toast to accompany hors d'oeuvres; a cheese board or plate with a bone or wooden handled cheese knife; a carving knife and fork, either matching the main set of cutlery or toning in style, and a selection of serving spoons — most canteens of cutlery include four or six of these. You may also like to acquire a serving slice for cutting and serving gâteaux and desserts. These are available in plain stainless steel and, much prettier,

in decorated plated silver. Danish and Swedish glass manufacturers make exquisite, flat, glass plates that are ideal for cheese or gâteaux.

Oven-to-table-ware
Specially toughened, oven-proof, glass dishes are useful for such foods as casseroles and stews and are generally acceptable on the table for less formal meals. Also available now is a wide variety of cream or white porcelain or stoneware dishes suitable for use in a conventional or microwave oven. These are of an attractive, simple design and blend well with most dinner services. Remember that dishes look much more attractive standing on a meat plate or large dinner plate that matches the main china, or standing on a coloured linen or paper napkin that fits the colour scheme. For deeper bowls or basins used for steak and kidney pudding or similar dishes a pretty linen napkin tied around the dish softens the effect of the plain, rather stark serving dish.

4 TABLE DECORATIONS

FLOWERS

It is important to start by choosing a colour scheme for the table setting and then to choose flowers that suit the style of the meal, the colour of the table linens, the china to be used and any candles to be placed on the table. The appearance of the room and the dinner table can be effectively varied by using flowers of different colours arranged in different ways. Several large arrangements of flowers can be placed around the room to echo the theme chosen for the table, and a much smaller arrangement should be used on the table itself. Tall vases and large spreading arrangements placed on the table are too intrusive and may mean that people cannot easily talk to each other across the table.

The table flower arrangement should be kept low and central, spreading gently outwards rather than upwards. The shape of the vase used is all important as it will affect the height of the flowers and the way they spread. Choose a low shallow vase and place inside a piece of crumpled chicken wire or oasis; this will hold the stems in place. For a really professional look each flower stem may be individually wired. Wire comes in various thicknesses according to the delicacy of the flower stem and for short stems a single wire can be cut in half with short scissors. The wire is pushed in near the flower head, bound to the stem with narrow green florists' tape which is stretchable and self-adhesive. The advantage of stem wiring is that you can gently move flower-heads or wired trails of leaves to create the desired effect without breaking delicate stems. All the necessary accessories are available at florists' shops.

Don't rule out the possibility of using containers other than vases for your flower arrangements. Old-fashioned milk jugs, antique glasses, cream jugs, interesting fruit bowls, stoneware jelly-moulds, pretty porcelain tea pots or coffee pots all make very suitable vases.

Keep small jars and bottles to make a basic arrangement which can be placed inside an unusual container. This is an added safeguard if the container itself is cracked or slightly damaged and liable to leak water on to furniture.

Caring for fresh flowers

When buying flowers, if you need an arrangement that is going to last, ask the florist for advice on flowers that will not wilt or drop their petals quickly. Some florists supply sachets of crystals that will ensure long life to cut flowers. If you want to create a stunning centre piece for just one evening, choose flowers that may not last very long but that are exactly the colour you need and that look more dramatic. It is possible to buy such flowers more cheaply.

Always ask the florist for advice on how best to care for flowers and never leave bunches of flowers lying around in their paper wrapping. As soon as possible, remove the wrapping and stand the flowers in a bucket of water until you have time to arrange them. Once in water, flowers prefer cool, airy rooms but they do need humidity and plenty of fresh cold water. To prevent wilting, make sure that the stems are well opened before placing in the vase. Using a slanting cut, snip the ends of soft stems and hammer the ends of woody stems, such as chrysanthemums, forsythia and roses. This enables them to absorb water more easily. Always remove leaves which will be left below the water level in the vase, as these will rot and pollute the water. Try not to position vases of flowers in a draught or too near a hot radiator. Finally, some flowers drink a lot of water, especially on hot days or in heated rooms. Do remember to top the water up otherwise they will dehydrate and droop.

Flowers picked from the garden should be plunged as soon as possible into a deep bucket of luke-warm water and left there for two to three hours. Floppy flowers, which bend their stems at the head, such as tulips, some roses, poppies etc., should be placed in a bucket with a thick layer of newspaper wrapped tightly around them. This will help to straighten the stem and make arranging easier. Blooms with fleshy stems, such as stocks and snapdragons, are better plunged into moderately hot water after shortening the stem by 1 cm (½ in) with a slanted cut.

Arranged for effect
If a small number of flowers are to be used as a table centre there are several ways of displaying them to their full advantage.

1 Snap off the flower heads and float the heads in a shallow bowl with leaves fanning out from underneath the petals. Japanese lotus bowls or rice bowls are ideal for one or more flower heads and are easily available from Japanese shops, or scour junk shops and antique markets for shallow glass or china vases that were made for this purpose.

2 Fix a house plant which has trailing foliage firmly in the centre of a pretty china bowl, deep enough to conceal the plant pot. Pack oasis or crumpled chicken wire around the pot, fill with water and arrange flowers around the pot, bringing out trailers from the plant between the flower heads. Choose plants and flowers that complement each other.

3 Place two or three flowers with a little fern or other foliage in a vase that has a narrow neck. This makes a delicate arrangement quite big enough for a small table. Or, use two or more such vases placed at opposite ends of a larger table.

4 Place single flower heads in small pretty glasses or bowls at each setting. Cocktail or liqueur glasses are ideal for this and if you are lucky enough to find art deco ones from the 1920s they will often be made from very beautiful, decorated, frosted or crackle glass.

CANDLES AND HOLDERS
Candles add elegance and romance to a table setting and throw a gentle light which is flattering to faces, flowers and food. Light a formal dinner with several candlesticks or use one or two candles for a more intimate romantic occasion.

The colour of the candles should be matched to china, linen and flowers and can be varied to suit different occasions. Red, white and green are ideal at Christmas, combined with holly, poinsettias and other festive items. A meal in springtime is brightened by daffodils and narcissi arranged with yellow, white and pale green candles. Try other colour combinations for different effects.

Candle shapes

Tall tapered candles are the most elegant and versatile in arrangements. They burn slowly and are very well suited to large arrangements or to stand on a buffet table or sideboard. Tall, very slim tapers, often called 'flower lights', suit delicate holders or Scandinavian-style flat candelabra. With several burning at once the effect is of a crown of light that is quite beautiful. Be careful about the positioning of these as they are not suitable in situations where food is to be handed over or round the table because of the danger of burns or damage to the candles or holders.

Chunky candles are not so elegant and therefore best used on less formal occasions or children's parties. They are sturdy and solid and burn very slowly, and children like them because they are often made in interesting shapes, such as cones, decorated pillars, animals and characters from favourite books and films. There are also novelty candles made to look like ice-cream sundaes and suchlike, which are great fun. Always position them in a place where they cannot be knocked over by children.

For parties, or special flower and candle arrangements, there are all sorts of fairy lights which burn for hours in their own holders and give a glow rather than a direct light. Small candles or night-lights can also be placed inside coloured glasses or large brandy glasses.

Floating candles are very pretty and have the added charm of the reflection in water of the flame. One kind that is available features a sherry-type glass with a wick and float and a special liquid that burns with a red or green flame.

Candle and flower arrangements

Candles and flowers look very attractive together and different arrangements can be suited to different seasons or to special festive occasions. For example, for autumn, fruits and vegetables can add a very effective touch, particularly such things as polished green or red peppers, avocado pears or aubergines. Arranged subtly with rich foliage, warm, glowing, flower colours and amber-coloured candles, the overall effect is of well-being, warmth and natural goodness.

For a christening, create a soft effect with pale blue or pink delicate flowers arranged with soft ferns and gypsophila. Choose pale pink, blue or white candles and add gently trailed furled white, pink or blue satin ribbons.

To create these arrangements you will need patience, inspiration and all sorts of useful materials — pin holders, Plasticine, florists' tape, wire, oasis, etc. The secret is in experimenting and practising until you find out what works and what gives the best overall effect.

Candle holders

Holders that take one or two candles are usually called candlesticks, and multiple candle holders, candelabra. Most people associate candelabra with a large multi-branched object but there are simpler, more modest designs. Some, less than 12 cm (4¾ in) high, are suitable for the dining-table but larger ones look particularly good on a sideboard or buffet-table.

It is important to choose candle holders that suit

the decor and the table setting. Small Scandinavian-style glass holders will look lost and out of place on a large formal dinner-table set for twenty-four people. Equally a pair of tall silver candelabra will not suit a family dinner-table set for Sunday lunch. Try to match the size and style of holders and candles to the occasion, decor, table size, and the position they are to occupy. Decide also whether one or two candles are enough, or whether you need more than this.

When you are arranging the candles make sure they are firmly fixed. This may mean shaving a little wax from the butt end to ensure that it fits the holder, or you may need to wind paper or card round the butt if the holder is a little too big.

Finally, some candlesticks are improved by having fresh, dried or silk flowers wound round the base. Rings of silk and dried flowers are available in the shops, and these slip over the top of the holder. Alternatively, fresh flowers may be wired and wound around the base of the candlestick or fixed winding up it. This is particularly effective if modern, plain-coloured, porcelain candlesticks are used, as the flowers soften the rather austere effect of the china.

Candle safety
Be very careful that candle holders are able to support the weight of the candles and that arrangements are not top heavy and liable to fall. Make sure that candles are not standing on wobbly tables or in a position where they are likely to be jogged in a crowded room. If you stand candles on a buffet-table against a window or wall, make sure they are well away from curtains and the wall itself. If part of a flower arrangement, make sure that any foliage is well away from burning candles.

OTHER DECORATIVE EFFECTS
If there is a special theme to your dinner party or buffet, you may want to add other items to the table setting. For example, for an engagement party, St Valentine's dinner or a wedding breakfast, little red hearts could be cut from shiny paper and stuck or pinned to the table cloth. Table mats could be made specially in the shape of a heart.

For Hallowe'en, a black witch's hat decorated with yellow stars and moons would make an ideal centre piece. Black candles, dark, purple-green foliage and artificial flowers could be worked into a very suitable black-magic style table decoration.

For a breakfast or brunch party use amusing egg-cups for boiled eggs and second-hand or modern, novelty cruet sets in the shape of tomatoes or pigs or ducklings. Light-hearted china helps start the day off well and keeps guests amused!

With a great deal of imagination and planning, interesting effects can be created for any occasion. Plan the menu, table setting and extra touches according to season, event and the mood you want to create. The extra effort involved will add to the enjoyment. There are plenty of ideas for celebrating all sorts of occasions in style in Chapter 7.

Place-cards and menus
These are fun to write out and can be used as another way of adding a special touch to the table. Place-cards are useful if you are entertaining more than six people. It stops people from milling around the table trying to decide where to sit, or waiting to be told. It is usual to seat men and women alternately, without placing husbands beside wives, if possible. The most important thing to bear in mind is to encourage a successful balance of lively and quiet personalities.

16   *Place card design for a wedding*

17   *Place card design for Christmas dinner*

To make the cards, use a thin firm card of a suitable colour to match the linens and china, fold in half lightly across the middle and write each name on the lower half of the folded card. Depending on the formality or informality of the occasion, use titles or Christian names accordingly. Decorate the card with symbols or drawings to suit the occasion and place towards the centre of the table close enough to the place-setting to leave no doubt as to who is sitting where.

When writing out the menu, below the title and date, centre the names of dishes one under the other with a space between courses. For an informal evening keep it light-hearted and interesting, using descriptive wording for each delicious dish, so as to whet your guests' appetite. For fun, give the dishes names to suit the event. For a Guy Fawkes Supper, how about 'Catherine Wheels' for canapés served with drinks, and 'November Casserole'; or for a children's Hallowe'en Party, 'Witch's Stew' and 'Wizard's Magic Pudding'!

Decorate the border of the menu with suitable pictures or symbols, such as holly leaves, Father Christmasses and snowmen for a Christmas meal; roses, marigolds and daisies for a midsummer luncheon. These can be linked with place-cards.

5 TABLE SETTING TECHNIQUES

CHOOSING TABLEWARE

Different styles of glassware, china and cutlery need to be very carefully mixed. A general rule is to use silver cutlery and cut glass with fine china; stainless steel and simple glassware with stoneware or pottery; china from a particular period with cutlery and glassware from the same period, if possible, or reproduction pieces that echo the style.

When trying to decide what to use, think of the following: is the colour scheme subtle or bold? Does the china and linen give a delicate or substantial effect? If subtle and delicate, use glassware and cutlery that fit in with this. Choose pieces that have fine, graceful, elegant shapes and only a little ornamentation. If the effect is bold and substantial, chunky modern glasses and heavier cutlery will blend better. Try to achieve a balance between all the different accessories you use.

Decide also whether you want a sparkling or more muted effect. For brightness and sparkle, well-polished silver and crystal glasses give a brilliant reflection to any lighting you use, particularly candle-light. To add more shine and light, you could choose silver goblets instead of glasses.

Bronze cutlery gives a gentler golden glow to a table setting and solid pewter and satin-finished steel with plain glassware give a quieter but pleasant gleam. The most muted, quiet effect is that of wood — wooden-handled cutlery, wooden cruet sets, wooden salad bowls and a bare polished wood table are suitable for informal, unfussy luncheons or for quick meals at home, but do not lend themselves to more elegant occasions.

COLOUR SCHEMES

The choice between buying patterned and plain china is often a difficult one. By buying china in a very unusual colour, or a particularly strong design, you may find you are restricted in the variety of effects you can create. It is a good idea to build up two services which will add to flexibility — one plain and one patterned; one for use on special occasions, one for more everyday use.

If a plain self-coloured china is too stark, choose an embossed design or a plain colour with a simple coloured rim or border which adds interest. The colour or colours from the rim can be picked out in the colour of tablecloths, napkins and flowers.

Here are a few ideas on matching patterned china to linens:

1 Strongly-patterned china looks best set on a plain cloth which matches one of the colours in the pattern, or which echoes the colour in a lighter or darker shade. It need not necessarily be the predominant colour. For example if there is a yellow

White lace over a yellow cloth forms a perfect background for the coloured cutlery and china for an informal spring lunch

centre to flowers in the pattern, the table-cloth could be of a toning yellow.

2 Patterned china featuring only two colours, such as an all-over pattern of blue and white, can be set on a patterned cloth of the same two colours but preferably in a geometric, simple pattern if the china has a flowered or abstract pattern. Napkins could be plain blue or white.

3 A two-colour scheme can be achieved by laying an open-weave white or cream lace table-cloth over a plain, coloured cloth. The china may echo both colours or only one, and the colours should extend to the flowers and candles used for the decorations.

4 All coloured china, patterned or plain, looks wonderful on a plain or lacy white linen cloth. Napkins should pick up one or more of the colours in the china and the same colours could be echoed in your choice of flowers and greenery, and possibly candles.

When using plain china try these combinations:

1 Lay the china on a plain cloth which gives a stunning colour contrast, for example, black china on a white cloth, or bright yellow on blue. Make napkins from a fabric that repeat the two colours.

2 Leave the table-top bare and use large, patterned, place mats. These may be heat-proof or laid over heat-proof mats. You may find that the mats come with matching napkins, but if not, make some in one of the stronger colours used in the mats.

3 Place a small brightly coloured plain or patterned cloth over a larger plain cloth in a toning colour. Napkins should echo the colour of the larger cloth.

4 White china is the most versatile and looks good on any kind of coloured cloth or on pretty place mats on a polished table surface.

SETTING THE TABLE

Leave yourself plenty of time as there are always little jobs to do to ensure that everything looks perfect. First decide which accessories you are going to use. Sometimes a cloth or napkins need ironing, using a little spray starch to give a fresh, crisp look. Silver and glasses may need polishing, mats may need a wipe over, flowers may have to be picked and so on.

Lay the table with the cloth or mats first. Count out the cutlery you need and set this next. Then come the glasses, well polished and sparkling. Count out the pieces of china you need for all the courses and stack ready in the kitchen, other than those you need for the first course and any side plates, which will go directly on the table.

Cutlery

The most important aspect of table setting is the positioning of the cutlery. The general rules are not as rigid as they used to be, but it is very important that forks go on the left and knives and spoons on the right, and that guests should be able to tell, by working from the outside inwards, which implements to use for which course.

The different settings for different menus are shown on pages 34 and 35. The setting for a meal consisting of soup, meat, pudding and cheese are shown in fig. 22. On the right, working inwards, are the bread knife, soup spoon, knife for the main meat course and spoon for the pudding. On the left are the forks for the main course and the pudding. If the first course is to be eaten with a fork, the soup spoon is left out and replaced by a small fork on the left of the main meat fork. The forks should be positioned with their prongs pointing upwards and the knives with their blades inwards.

18 *A snack lunch (soup)*

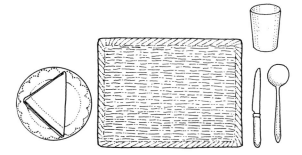

19 *Informal lunch*

20 *Family meal*

21 *Modern style family lunch*

22 *Family celebration dinner*

23 *Five course dinner for guests*

24 *Four course dinner for guests*

It is quite correct, but less formal, to position the pudding spoon and fork, or teaspoon for ice-cream, above the setting, as in fig. 20. This positioning has the advantage of saving space.

At a formal dinner, if there is a dessert, such as fresh fruit, a dessert knife and fork are brought in on the dessert plate with a finger-bowl.

To soften a very formal setting the bread knife can be positioned on top of the folded napkin on the side plate, as in fig. 23. Likewise, the cutlery needed for an hors d'oeuvre other than soup, may be laid on the plate ready for eating – for example, a grapefruit spoon on a small plate next to the grapefruit half in a sundae dish; or a small fork or spoon next to a prawn cocktail in a wine glass on a small plate. This course is placed on top of the plate which will be used for the second course.

Plates

If there is no course between the hors d'oeuvre and the main one, the largest rather than the medium-sized plate should be set under it, unless you intend to bring in the main course ready served, or to set warmed plates for it. It is much better to serve hot food on warmed plates.

Glasses

At most dinner parties only one wine is served and the glass should be positioned just above the blade of the large knife. If more than one wine is to be served the glasses should be positioned in the order they will be used, working from right to left, the furthest away being used first, or in a triangular pattern. It is a good idea to have a jug of iced water or a carafe of iced mineral water on the table and to give water goblets as required.

The finishing touches

Once all the necessary items are laid out on the table, stand back and decide where to position salt and pepper pots, bread baskets, place cards (if being used), mats for serving dishes (unless you plan to serve from the sideboard or trolley), butter dishes and flowers. If the central flower, or flower and candle, decoration is already in position, look at the height of the glasses. Is the balance right? Tall slender candles look better with long-stemmed fine glasses than with squat chunky ones. Are the flowers too tall? Is the table too cramped? If the space on the table is limited you could dispense with a bread basket and place rolls and pats of butter ready on each side plate. The napkins can be folded into a mitre shape and placed in the glasses.

Instead of a central flower arrangement that may take up too much room, place single flowers floating in finger bowls or glasses at each place setting, or use small sprays of flowers to decorate each rolled napkin.

Finally, check that salt and pepper pots are filled, that chairs are in position, lighting is organized – and to avoid the risk of fire, that candles forming part of the central arrangement are stable, and are not touching leaves, ribbons or flowers.

6 EVERYDAY OCCASIONS

BREAKFAST

If entertaining guests to breakfast, position the table in the sunniest spot so as to get the day off to a good start. If the weather is bad or you do not have a sunny spot, lay the table with a bright sunny cloth and colourful china.

For a full breakfast you will need cereal bowls, side plates, tea or coffee cups and saucers, cereal spoons, knives and forks or small spoons for boiled eggs, small knives for buttering toast, toast racks, teaspoons and napkins. Grapefruit halves are usually served in small dishes, ready segmented with a knife, with special pointed spoons. Put out milk in jugs (hot to accompany coffee), sugar in a pretty bowl, jars of jam and marmalade, salt and pepper shakers, and pots of tea or coffee.

The breakfast tray

Lay a clean embroidered tray cloth on a large sturdy tray. Lay a place for one with whatever food is to be offered. Arrange a small teapot or coffee pot, milk jug, sugar bowl, salt and pepper, and dish of butter for toast at one side, and at the other a small narrow-necked vase with one or two fresh flowers, any letters and a folded news-paper. It is not really practical to provide hot crispy bacon or fried eggs unless a large tray is used with enough room for a covered dish to keep the food hot!

BRUNCH

If you have a garden and the weather permits, brunch parties in the garden are great fun. Serve Buck's Fizz or plain orange juice in tall glasses and serve special food, such as devilled kidneys or scrambled eggs with prawns or smoked salmon. The table setting is the same as for breakfast with the addition of flowers in the centre or a large bowl of fruit.

LUNCH

For a family lunch or informal lunch for friends, the table setting will obviously depend on the sort of food being served. The meal might be simply a bowl of soup with crusty bread and cheese, in which case a very simple table setting will be sufficient. A meal of this kind may well be eaten at the kitchen table, but it is nice to arrange the table attractively and with care, using linen or pretty paper napkins and pretty mats – if not a table-cloth.

AFTERNOON TEA

This is rather different from the conventional place setting of other formal meals, as the individual settings consist of only a small plate, a folded napkin and a cake fork or small knife, if cakes or hot buttered muffins or tea-cakes, which need cutting, are on the menu. Spread a colourful table-cloth on

The floral theme from the blinds and the window box is carried through with the lightly decorated china

the table before setting it and place your best cups and saucers, with teaspoons, in front of you, with a jug of milk, a little plate of lemon slices, a tea-strainer, if loose-leafed tea is used, the pot of tea and a jug of hot water, both standing on heat-proof mats. A bowl of white sugar should be handed round as necessary. If sugar-cubes are used, tongs should be provided.

Arrange plates of neat sandwiches, sliced bread and butter, scones, toasted muffins or crumpets around the outer part of the table so that guests can help themselves. Jams and honey should be served in pretty glass or china jam pots with spoons. Antique shops and junk markets are excellent places to find extremely pretty second-hand jam pots, some with silver lids, some with matching spoons. Pretty china jam and honey pots brighten up the tea-table enormously. In the centre of the table place fancy cakes, biscuits, gâteaux and fruit loaves, each arranged on a paper doily on serving plates that match or tone with the tea-set.

For an informal tea, when guests sit in armchairs rather than round the table, you should have a low table or trolley beside you with all the necessary tea things and the cups and saucers. Hand a cup of tea to each guest, offering milk, lemon and sugar and make sure that everyone has a small plate and a folded napkin. There should be a low table placed close to each arm-chair large enough to take the guest's plate and teacup.

The sort of food you offer should be easy to eat without forks and knives and it is a good idea to display sandwiches and cakes on a three-tier cake stand so that guests can see what is still to come. To make the room attractive, lay pretty lace table-cloths or mats over the small tables and place vases of fresh flowers around the room.

HIGH TEA

As high tea is a much more informal, family affair than afternoon tea, your everyday china is quite suitable. An unfussy practical setting is required, with a fairly plain table-cloth set with everyday cutlery. As hot dishes are usually served, each place setting should include a large knife and fork as well as a side plate and small knife for spreading butter and jam.

SNACK MEALS

If a very light meal is to be eaten after the theatre or in the early evening a low occasional table is ideal for arranging dishes and setting informal places. Almost any 'snack' meal can be served in this way. If the surface is not heat-proof, any hot plates of food and coffee pots should be placed either on a heat-proof tray or large mat.

DINNER

This can vary from an informal evening meal with two or three courses to a full dinner with five or six courses, and the table setting will vary accordingly. Stick to the golden rules and techniques discussed in Chapter 9 and it should be possible to create the right mood and style to suit the occasion. Part of the secret of a successful dinner party is that it should run smoothly, and if you have planned well beforehand and have worked out how to serve the different courses, you should not have too many problems.

Serving

When tables were larger and most dinners included a huge roast joint of meat, it was quite usual for the host to carve and serve individual portions on to a pile of hot plates in front of him, while the hostess served vegetables and sauces at the other end of the table. For this to work a servant was needed to carry plates back and forth. Nowadays, it is quite normal to place vegetable dishes, sauce boats and salad bowls on the table in front of guests. The host or hostess serves the main dish and hands a plate to each guest, who then serves him or herself to vegetables. This method suits modern menus much better since the meal might consist of a casserole with rice, or a selection of Indian or Chinese dishes and it is much easier for people to help themselves.

Alternatively the host or hostess serves all the vegetables or accompanying dishes from a hotplate on the sideboard and carries a filled plate to each guest. A heated hostess trolley is another useful aid. A hotplate is an excellent investment as all the vegetables and sauces and even the main dish can be kept hot until second helpings are required.

If there is no room for dishes on the table and no sideboard or similar piece of furniture, food can be dished up in the kitchen and filled plates brought quickly through and placed in front of each guest. If a salad is to be served, it is usual to place the salad bowl and dressing on the table at the same time as the main course. Some people may eat salad with the hot food while others like to serve it on a separate side plate afterwards. Have small plates ready to replace any used for salad, so that guests have them ready for the cheese course. If you have individual bowls for salad, place these on the table outside the place setting on the left, to balance the glasses on the right.

7 SPECIAL OCCASIONS

For any special occasion, whether it is a candle-lit dinner for two, a summer barbecue for friends, or a celebration dinner decide what effect you wish to create – think of the colour scheme carefully, plan the food and drink to suit the occasion, then add any suitable trimmings to set the whole thing off to full advantage.

A ROMANTIC TABLE FOR TWO

For a romantic, intimate meal, a small square or round table is essential. The ideal position for the table is on a balcony, a roof garden, terrace or patio, but if these settings are not available choose a spot indoors that will help create a romantic mood – near a french window overlooking the garden, in a corner of a room uncluttered by everyday objects.

The only effective form of lighting for such an occasion is candlelight. Indoors, one or two tall elegant candles are enough; outdoors a candle burning inside a glass is better, so as to protect the gentle flame from the breeze. The candles will throw a soft, flattering glow, enveloping the romantic couple in a private circle of light.

Decorate the table simply and delicately, with a small arrangement of fragile flowers. Use white or pastel shades for linens and your very best china and glassware. Plan a menu that can be prepared beforehand so that you only have to serve the food, not spend precious time between courses cooking and serving. You should be able to spend as much time as possible with your guest and you should be relaxed and unflustered by frantic activity behind the scenes.

A BUFFET

A buffet meal is ideal for occasions where there is to be a large number of guests such as christenings, weddings and similar gatherings. It may also suit a smaller gathering such as an informal supper with friends after the theatre or an evening at home where a dinner around the table might be more formal than you want to make it.

When planning the table arrangements and flowers or other decorations, think carefully about a colour scheme or theme to suit the occasion. For example, if the meal you are planning is to celebrate a silver wedding, choose white flowers with silvery foliage, silver candles or white candles in silver candlesticks and trimmings of furled silver ribbons. Silver serving dishes and silver cutlery will help to set the scene and if you don't have these yourself, you can hire, or possibly borrow, them. If the occasion is a christening, you will probably choose pink or blue as the predominant colour, and flowers should be delicate and unfussy.

Dried flowers are used here to echo the delicate flower print of the table-cloth and the colours of the china and cutlery

The next most important decision is where to place the table.

Buffet-table set against the wall. This gives more space in the room itself but limits the number of people who can help themselves to food at one time. So, work out a simple plan of where to position food, plates, cutlery, etc., to help prevent collisions and over-crowding.

It sometimes helps to repeat the arrangements of dishes starting at both ends of the table and meeting in the middle, or if the party is spreading into two rooms, set up a table in each room with the same selection of food on each.

Keep decorative arrangements of flowers, candles, fruit, etc, to the back of the table and dishes of food easily accessible at the front, with plenty of serving spoons and forks. For occasions when there is a celebration cake, either position the cake as the central focus of attention on the main table or place it on a separate table with a vase of flowers and a silver knife.

Buffet-table placed away from the wall. More people can serve themselves, so there is less likelihood of congestion and collision. However, the arrangement of the table is a little more complicated because it must look good from every angle. The flower decorations or decorative bowl of fruit or cake must be central and vases and candlesticks can stand at each end, well away from the edge. Place stacks of plates, napkins and cutlery in low piles at either end of the table. If there is a hot dish, place it at one end of the table and continue, using one side of the table, with salads, sauces, bread and desserts to the far end. On the other side of the table, begin with the cold main dish, if there is one, at the opposite end from the hot dish, and continue through to the desserts.

This method allows guests to approach the table from opposite ends on both sides. Try to persuade guests to serve themselves a few at a time so that there is not a huge crowd all trying to get to the food at the same time. If necessary fill up dishes as the meal progresses or have duplicate dishes ready in the kitchen to bring out when necessary.

It is usually much better to serve drinks from a separate table or sideboard. Place pretty mats on every surface around the room so that glasses can be put down without spoiling furniture or paintwork. When planning the menu, try to limit the food to items that can be eaten with only a fork or the fingers. It is impossible to juggle knife, fork, plate and glass at the same time. Desserts, too, should be the kind that are easily eaten with just a fork or just a spoon. Remove dirty plates and dishes as soon as possible to the kitchen so that the table still looks neat, pretty and inviting. Towards the end of the meal, clear one end of the table to make room for coffee and coffee cups.

CATERING FOR LARGE NUMBERS

It is not usually necessary to hire professional caterers or florists to create a table setting for a big occasion. You may need to hire trestle tables which can be covered with lightly-starched white sheets and if you don't have enough table-cloths, use disposable cloths. China, cutlery and glassware can also be hired and although this limits your choice of style and type of china, plain white china or white with a gold or coloured rim is usually available and can be dressed up to suit the occasion. (For further advice see Chapter 8, page 46.)

A GARDEN PARTY

A garden party is merely a buffet out of doors, so the planning of flowers, table arrangements and food is the same. Because of the risk of bad weather a marquee is often hired and the buffet meal is usually set up inside. As this sort of event is usually held in mid-summer, there will probably be plenty of brightly-coloured flowers to use for table decorations and quantities of summer fruit to include in the menu.

If the weather is very hot you may need to put up garden umbrellas to provide shade for guests. Under each, place a small table and a group of chairs. Cover the tables with pretty table-cloths and place tiny vases of flowers on each, leaving as much space as possible for glasses and plates of food to be put down.

A TABLE IN THE GARDEN

The style and mood you choose to create will depend largely on whether you are planning an informal family affair or a more elegant dinner for guests. If it is to be a family occasion, place a pretty jug filled with fresh flowers cut from the garden in the middle of the table. If you have a big, old-fashioned pine table lay the china directly on to it. Alternatively cover the table with a bright, cheerful cloth with either matching linen or paper napkins. Keep the setting unfussy but bright and pretty.

For a more formal dinner, spread the table with a white or pale cream cloth, or you may like to use disposable cloths. There is a very good selection of attractive disposable tableware now available in shops. Use café clips to hold cloths firmly to the edge of the table to stop them from blowing in the breeze. Decorate the table with delicate vases of flowers and place candles, protected by glass holders, at intervals along the table. Garden flares are ideal for lighting such an occasion held in the evening.

Keep the menu simple and easy to serve, otherwise the host or hostess will spend an awful lot of time walking to and from the kitchen to collect dishes. Cold food is obviously easiest, and as such occasions are likely to be held in summer, make the most of salads and fresh fruit.

BARBECUES

These are the ideal occasions for using some of the extremely attractive disposable tableware now available – plates, napkins, throw-away glasses or cups and even brightly-coloured plastic cutlery. A barbecue is by nature an informal, family affair, where children can help cook and serve the food, so don't use precious dishes or plates that might get broken. Stick to very practical, hard-wearing dishes and kitchen utensils. For a large number of guests arrange chairs and small tables around the garden and cover with very brightly coloured paper table-cloths, and use plates, napkins, cutlery, cups or plastic glasses in the same bright colours. For evening barbecues, place garden flares around the garden to give plenty of light. Set up a sturdy table near the barbecue where sauces, mustards, dips, bread and suitable drinks for both adults and children can be placed. Have a pile of plates ready so that food can be served as soon as it is ready.

PICNICS

Picnics don't need to just be made up of a few sandwiches, cold sausages and pies, etc. They can be quite elaborate meals, beautifully set out and all the more tasty for being eaten in the open air.

For a summer picnic, take salads, mixed ready in air-tight plastic boxes or even china bowls, if there is room for these to travel safely; barbecued chicken legs, ham wrapped around asparagus spears; fresh

An Italian-style supper party; uncooked strips of canelloni form unusual napkin holders

crusty bread or pitta bread ready to fill with mayonnaise; cheese; cold meats; vegetable mixes; and sauces.

If you have a good sturdy picnic basket or hamper, pack it with china plates and either metal or disposable cutlery, real or throw-away glasses, pretty napkins and essentials such as salt and pepper, a corkscrew, butter knives, a tin opener, bread knife, spreading knives and serving spoons.

You will need either a picnic table and folding chairs, or a waterproof cover for the ground and a rug or thick cloth to go over it. Lay the food out on a pretty table-cloth and let people help themselves.

For a winter picnic, you might want to have a small camp-fire burning (if you are allowed to) and some of the food could be cooked – you could fry sausages, toast bread, cook baked potatoes in the embers, toast marshmallows and even boil the kettle for tea!

COCKTAIL PARTIES

Cocktail parties usually take place in the evening before dinner, from 6 p.m. until 8 or 8.30 p.m. Invitations can be as formal or informal and as original as you like, and the party may be as simple or elaborate as you wish to make it. You may choose to serve one alcoholic drink only, for example, sherry or champagne, or wine, or you may decide to serve a variety of cocktails (be sure that you are well versed in making them), spirits or aperitifs. Soft drinks should also be available. Whatever the drinks you offer, have glasses the right shape to serve them in.

Choose 1930s-style glasses for cocktails and have ready suitable items to place in the drinks; olives, sliced lemon or baby onions for dry drinks, maraschino cherries for sweet drinks. If you use tall glasses decorate the rim of the glass with elaborate arrangements of sliced apples, oranges, lemons and then push a baby paper parasol into the fruit to top it all. Novelty ice cubes and straws are also fun, and altogether the party can be very colourful.

Decorate the room with plenty of flowers, making sure you leave ample space for dishes of food, glasses and ashtrays to be put down. Decide where you want the drinks table or 'bar' to be, and if using a table, cover it with a decorated cloth (either linen or disposable). If there is room, place a small vase of flowers in one corner and make sure you have all the various bottles you need. You will also need bottle openers, corkscrews and miniature napkins. It is a good idea to place little piles of napkins around the room so that they are easily accessible.

Food should be light and simple and should be presented so that it can be easily eaten with fingers. Serve bowls filled with a selection of mixed nuts (not just peanuts); stuffed olives and other cocktail pickles (onions, gherkins, etc.); baby sandwiches and canapés (these need to be extremely fresh when served as they dry very quickly, so don't prepare them too soon in advance of the party); dips with sliced vegetables and a range of crisps, tortillas, corn chips; baby sausages on sticks; little savoury flans and vol au vents filled with shrimps or chicken.

Lay dishes of food around the room, and at times circulate with them or ask a friend to take them round. Make sure that there are plenty of mats on tables so that glasses can be put down without damaging furniture.

8   CELEBRATE IN STYLE

A WEDDING RECEPTION

The most important aspect of a wedding reception is that it should be very enjoyable. Whether the meal is a formal seated affair or a buffet, everything should run calmly and smoothly and everybody should be very relaxed. This is why most people put the whole affair into the hands of outside caterers who will do all the worrying and hard work for them. However, it is not impossible to organize a reception yourself and still be a relaxed guest or member of the family party. Do get as much help as you can, however – waiters, wine waiters and kitchen help are almost essential.

The first consideration when planning the table layout is the colour scheme. The colour of table decorations, the cake and any flowers on the cake must tone with the bride's dress and bouquet and the bridesmaids' dresses. If the cake is to be decorated with fresh flowers they should be a variation on the bride's bouquet so that the bride's flowers can be placed by the cake during the reception and tone exactly. If the cake is decorated with sugar flowers and ribbons, they too must match the bride's colour scheme exactly.

For a formal dinner or lunch, the flower decorations on the tables should be low, delicate arrangements that echo the bouquet with perhaps a slightly more elaborate arrangement on the head table. Table-cloths and napkins should be white and the cutlery silver. Crystal glass looks very elegant but the choice of design is a personal one and may be dictated by the hire company or catering organization who are responsible for the reception.

For a buffet, choose food that is light, elegant and easy to eat with the fingers or just a fork. (For layout of food, etc., see pages 40 to 43.) Arrange food delicately so that it looks appetizing, and remember to garnish with contrasting colours such as little sprigs of parsley, cucumber twists, tiny bunches of mustard and cress, tomato lilies or twists of lemon or orange. It is always amazing what a difference a simple garnish makes to the presentation of food. If there are to be children at the reception remember to plan the menu so that there is something to suit their tastes.

As for drinks, sometimes wine is served with the buffet meal and then champagne is served when the cake is to be cut. Alternatively, champagne is served throughout. Remember to have soft drinks available for children or adults who don't drink alcohol.

When planning a layout of the buffet table, decide carefully where the cake is to be positioned. It should either be the centre of attention on the main buffet table or it should be on a separate table.

If on a separate table, decorate this table with flowers that match the colour scheme, and place the cake on an elegant silver cake stand (these can be hired), with a silver-handled knife ready for the cutting ceremony later.

The main buffet-table can be decorated quite elaborately with flowers and swathes of ribbons. But don't make the decorations so elaborate that people can't get to the food, and keep table decorations to the centre area of the table.

Here are some ideas for decorating large buffet-tables. These can be adapted to suit other occasions where you may want to include special items to fit a chosen theme. (See silver and gold wedding anniversary, page 48.)

1 Swags can be used to decorate the front of the table. These are made of rolled florist's ribbon, looped and held to the edge of the table with drawing-pins. Bunches of roses (stems placed in damp cottonwool and wrapped in foil cones) are then pinned to the cloth to cover the drawing-pins. Fix garlands of more ribbon from the top of the cake to the back corners.

25-27 *Three ways to decorate a buffet-table for a wedding*

25

2 Make loops of different lengths using four strands of ribbon 2.5 cm (1 in) wide, pinned to the edge of the table. Bunches of dried or paper flowers with a few silver leaves are then fixed to hide the drawing-pins. If you have a coloured cloth, use white ribbons and flowers.

26

3 Pin looped Smilax creeper to the edge of the table. Add bows of white or coloured ribbon with long trailing ends and fix to hide the pins. To make swags and garlands, attach bunches of Smilax (order in advance from a florist) to a thin rope with Sellotape – grading the thickness of the swags.

Using drawing pins or other methods of fastening decorations securely to the table, of course only applies to trestle tables concealed by cloths.

27

A WEDDING ANNIVERSARY

To celebrate a wedding anniversary in style it is a fun idea to take as the theme the symbol that represents the particular number of years a couple has been married. The first few are a bit of a joke but as the number of years of marriage increases so the anniversary symbol becomes more valuable and romantic. They are:

One year: Cotton.
Two years: Paper.
Three years: Leather.
Four years: Fruit and flowers.
Five years: Wood.
Six years: Sugar and Sweets.
Seven years: Wool.
Eight years: Bronze.
Nine years: Pottery.
Ten years: Tin.
Eleven years: Steel.
Twelve years: Silk.
Thirteen years: Lace.
Fourteen years: Ivory.
Fifteen years: Crystal.
Twenty years: China.
Twenty-five years: Silver.
Thirty years: Pearl or Ivory.
Thirty-five years: Coral.
Forty years: Ruby.
Forty-five years: Sapphire.
Fifty years: Gold.
Fifty-five years: Emerald.
Sixty years: First Diamond.
Seventy-five years: Second Diamond.

The anniversaries that are most commonly celebrated by a gathering of family and friends are twenty-five years (silver) and fifty years (gold).

A formal dinner

If the anniversary is to be celebrated by a formal dinner the table or tables should be covered with white damask or white lace and laid with the very best china and cutlery. Spend some time on planning the flower arrangements as these should be very special. For a silver wedding choose white flowers — lilies, white roses, marguerite daisies, white poppies and silver foliage. If the arrangement includes candles, choose long delicate white tapers or silver candles. Choose silver vases or rose bowls for flower arrangements and trail furls of delicate silver ribbon in amongst the flowers, around the candlesticks or over the sides of the vase. For a gold wedding choose yellow and white flowers — not dull yellows but light, bright colours, such as daffodils, narcissi, or pale tea-roses — and ivy foliage with yellow berries. If possible use gold candlesticks or choose gold candles arranged with the flowers, and use golden trailing ribbons to trim the arrangement. Grasses, twigs or foliage can be sprayed with a silver or gold spray paint to form the background of the flower arrangement, or choose large leaved foliage, such as magnolia or camelia and add a touch of silver or gold spray paint to their edges.

You might like to employ extra help for the cooking and serving. As it is such a special occasion it is very much better if all the family and friends celebrating can relax and leave the work to someone else. If you are going to leave all the serving to helpers, brief them thoroughly beforehand. Go through the details of each course, how it is to be served and garnished, which wines are to be served with each course, whether there are to be any speeches or toasts and, if so, when (as this will affect the final preparation and presentation of any courses or anniversary cake that are to follow).

An elegant, period flavour is created by cleverly toning stylish, modern cutlery with china and glassware made in 1930's style

If champagne is to be poured, decide when, and make sure that everybody has a glass before toasts are made.

If you don't have any help, plan the meal very carefully so that there is an absolute minimum of work to be done between courses. Prepare as much as you can in advance, and make a very careful work plan so that everything runs smoothly on the day.

A buffet celebration

If a buffet celebration is preferred and you plan to invite a large number of guests, you may need to hire large trestle tables and cover them with white cloths. Serving dishes and plates can be decorated with silver or gold paper doilies. As well as placing flower arrangements on the table (see above for suggestions) decorate the edge of the table with garlands and ribbons (see illustrations on page 47). Use flowers of the appropriate colour and include silver or gold wedding bells, horseshoes or other decorations to suit the particular anniversary.

Again you may like to employ waiters or waitresses to hand round the food and drinks. The host and hostess are then free to chat with their guests and enjoy the party without constantly worrying about serving.

Try to create a menu with really special things that make the entire occasion a real treat. Don't forget to garnish each dish with a colourful touch to make everything really attractive. Here are a few ideas for the type of food to serve at a special anniversary buffet:

Canapés with cream cheese and caviar.

Smoked salmon pinwheels: made by spreading brown bread with a salmon mousse, lay slices of smoked salmon on top, roll up, chill, then slice.

Vol au vents filled with prawns.

Fresh salmon garnished with wafer-thin slices of cucumber.

King prawns wrapped in bacon and grilled.

Rich chicken liver pâté on dainty pieces of toast.

Celery hearts filled with blue cheese blended with butter.

Mussel shells filled with mussels combined with mayonnaise and chopped parsley.

Dainty tartlets filled with creamed chicken or shrimps in a creamy sauce.

Honey-roast ham wrapped around slices of avocado pear or asparagus tips.

A CHILDREN'S PARTY

Children's parties should be fun and lively and very much geared to the particular likes of the child whose birthday it is. One of the best ways of creating an entertaining, lively atmosphere is to choose a theme which follows through from the invitations to the table decorations, food, drinks and even all the party games.

Decide first on a theme by discussing with the birthday boy or girl what they would like. They may have an interest or hobby that is the obvious topic; otherwise try and choose something that will give plenty of scope for games, fancy dress, a novelty cake, table decorations etc. Here are a few ideas: outer space; ghosts and monsters; castles and dungeons; a favourite television character; the circus; a Disney character; a visit to the Zoo.

Having decided on a theme, and having set the date and time, send out the invitations. You may find that there are commercially produced cards that fit your theme. If not, make your own by decorating a plain, coloured card with suitable pictures or drawings. For a monster party the cards could be cut out in the shape of an ugly monster face; for a circus party it could be a clown's face.

Next, decide on a cake. If you don't have the time or flair to make a novelty cake yourself, order one from the local cake shop or cake-maker in plenty of time. Almost anything is possible and there is a good range of books on the market to help you. For a Disney party, a Mickey Mouse cake or Donald Duck cake would be ideal; for a castles and dungeons party, create a castle with towers and fortifications; for a circus party, a clown or decorated elephant would be wonderful; for an outer space party, why not have a space rocket or space shuttle?

Then comes the menu. Decide what foods will suit the children who are coming, and try to create names for the food that fit into the theme. For example, for a space party, little meatballs stuck all over with potato chips could be 'meteorites'; and sandwiches cut with a star cutter could be 'shooting stars'. For a circus party, you could serve 'monkey nuts', 'giant's sandwiches' (made with four or five slices of bread put together one on top of the other with different fillings), and 'lion tamer's supplies' of sausages on sticks or hamburgers. The drinks can be given names too: 'inter-galactic fuel' for a space party; 'dragon's blood' for a castles and dungeons party, and so on. Get the children to help dream up the names.

The table layout should continue the theme of the party and you may need to raid the toy cupboard for this. If possible, use tableware that won't be damaged by the children. Better still, use disposable cloths, plates, cups, etc. There is a good range available, and if you can't find anything that fits your theme, buy plain paper cups and plates and decorate them yourselves. Choose a table-cloth in a suitable colour or design. For a Disney party use a paper table-cloth and draw some of the characters on, or stick cut-outs all over it. If you can find some models of Disney characters, build a scene on the table and place the cake in the middle as the focal point. For a space scene use a black or dark blue cloth (you can always dye an old sheet) and stick sputniks, stars and moons all over it and place the space shuttle cake in the middle. Or create a moonscape on a brown background and use models of astronauts, rockets, space creatures to build the scene. Buy or make table napkins to match the cloth or use white ones. For a space scene, roll them and stand them up like moon rockets; for a circus party create the clown hats illustrated in fig. 9 on page 15.

28 *A children's 'space party'*

Adapt standard games to fit the theme of the party. At a space party for example, simple charades could be based on the titles of relevant well-known films or television programmes which will be familiar to all the children present and therefore easy to guess.

29 *A children's 'circus party'*

Whatever you choose to do for your children's party, do remember that they make a mess – that they can get very excited and noisy and a little wilder than usual – so hold the party in the kitchen or the garden, if the weather is fine. Don't use furniture or china that will damage easily. If you do, and there's an accident, make light of it and don't ruin the party!

THEME PARTIES

Some of the most successful parties that are fun to organize are theme parties. These are variations on the fancy dress party. The idea is to choose a theme, for example: black and white; red and gold; hats; characters from musical shows; a desert island. Send out appropriate invitations in plenty of time so that your guests have the opportunity to dream up a costume, and then plan the decorations, food and drink so that the entire event follows the theme through.

Invitations can be home-made or, if commercially produced ones fit the theme, use them. For a stylish black and white party, all sorts of design ideas are possible: a silhouette cut-out of Fred Astaire in *Top Hat and Tails*; a chessboard with the words written in the white squares; two masks cut out side by side, one black, one white, with the details of the party on the back. Do state clearly whether the event is to be a dinner party or a larger, informal gathering, and insist on fancy dress.

On the day or evening of the party organize the table and room decorations. For a dinner party spread the table with a black cloth and white napkins or white cloth and black napkins; or you may be able to find printed patterned fabrics that offer a contrasting mixture. The flowers for the centre of the table could be fresh white flowers in a black vase or artificial black flowers, or even very deep red or purple fresh flowers in a white vase. Candles can be black in white candlesticks or the reverse. If you have black- or white-handled cutlery this will add to the effect and you may find among the range of glasses now available frosted white or dark grey wine glasses. If you are using place cards use black ink on white cards or white spirit pen on black card and decorate the cards accordingly.

A simple breakfast tray is set with crisp blue linen, forming a pretty background for the blue and white china

30 *A party based on a desert island theme*

For a buffet gathering, cover the table with a black cloth, or black crêpe paper, and decorate with twists of white crêpe paper with garlands in the two colours at each corner. Decorate the room with strands of black and white twisted crêpe paper. Use black and white dishes for the food. Place vases of white flowers around the room and have candles burning in safe places. Once all the guests have arrived in costume the overall effect will be stunning.

CHRISTMAS

The traditional colours for Christmas decorations are red, green and white with touches of silver and glitter to set a festive tone. Most people decorate the house with special Christmas effects and the Christmas dinner-table should fit in with the decorations used in the dining room. The simplicity of red is very effective, linking naturally with evergreens such as holly, poinsettias, mistletoe, Christmas roses and other greenery that is traditionally used to decorate the house. Scandinavian wooden figures in red, green and white look very pretty on the tree, and wooden candle holders in green and red with matching candles look really attractive, both around the room and on the dinner-table. Just a touch of narrow crinkly tinsel draped over the tree, over plants and picture frames is enough to give the whole room a seasonal glow.

For the centre of the Christmas dinner-table, fix bright red candles firmly into plasticine or oasis and surround the candles with clusters of greenery — ivy, holly, mistletoe and sprays of evergreen leaves. Use silver or red gift-wrap ribbon which can be curled and arranged to lie gently among the leaves and on to the table-cloth. Depending on the size of the table, either make one large centre decoration with four or five candles and plenty of foliage, or several smaller decorations with a single candle in amongst the greenery, to place at intervals along a long table. The table-cloth should be white in order to set off the red and green of the decorations, and choose napkins that complement the red and green theme — either paper napkins covered with Christmas designs or linen napkins in bright red or green. Tie linen napkins in a loose neat roll with curled silver, green or red ribbon, or secure lightly with a simple napkin ring and a sprig of mistletoe. Place silver or gold paper dishes full of Christmas bon-bons at intervals around the table. Crackers are usually too big and clumsy for the table, so either buy tiny ones for decoration or keep the big ones for later in the meal, when nuts, dates and other goodies appear. Before the meal begins, switch on the Christmas tree lights, light the candles and turn off the electric lights.

NEW YEAR

For a dinner party, set a festive scene by choosing a colour scheme that has a special, celebratory feel, for example: black, gold, and purple; red, white and gold; silver and pink. Gift-wrap ribbon is always ideal for creating festive, table-centre decorations as it can be curled into streamers, and trailed over or around table decorations. As it is shiny it reflects candle-light very effectively. Choose real or artificial flowers to fit your chosen theme; arrange candles and ribbons with the flowers to form the decorations for the table. Tie curled strands of ribbon around paper or linen napkins to add to the decorative effect.

If red, white and gold is to be your colour scheme, choose a white table-cloth and red napkins tied with gold and red ribbons. Place gold or red candles in an arrangement of gold-sprayed leaves, red roses or other bright red flowers mixed with white chrysanthemums. Trail gold and red curled ribbons in amongst the arrangement. Lay a flower at each guest's place – a red rose for the ladies and a white carnation for the men. Little gold bon-bon dishes with sugared almonds and red and gold-wrapped chocolates will help to fill gaps on the table. Place cards can be made from red card and written with thick gold lettering, and a menu can echo the theme with red lettering on gold card.

ST VALENTINE'S DAY

A special dinner party for St Valentine's Day may be a romantic dinner for two or a large gathering for friends. The theme that should run throughout for both table decorations and food is a red heart. If sending out invitations, cut out heart-shaped cards. Plan the food to include as many heart shapes as possible. Here are a few ideas:

Heart-shaped puff pastry cases filled with a creamy mixture of prawns or shrimps, grated lemon rind, lemon mayonnaise, chopped spring onions and cream.

Canapés of wholemeal bread covered with smoked salmon and cut with a heart-shaped cutter.

Sandwiches cut with a heart-shaped cutter, of wholemeal bread filled with cream cheese, chopped cucumber and diced red pepper.

Heart-shaped garnishes cut from red pepper or the skin of firm red tomatoes.

Heart-shaped meringues filled with whipped cream, brandy and crushed pineapple; or filled with cream, raspberries and Kirsch.

A large cake baked in a heart-shaped tin and decorated in white and red, with a large red rose on the top.

Dainty shortbreads or other biscuits cut with a heart-shaped cutter and sprinkled lightly with castor sugar.

31 *St Valentine's Day*

The table should be laid with a white cloth — or you may be able to find a commercially-produced cloth printed with little red hearts. Fold lacy napkins into a heart shape (see fig. 8, page 14) and place a small red rose on each napkin. Decorate the table with an elaborate vase of red roses, or press heads of anemonies, roses and carnations into an oasis cut into a heart-shape. Trail curled, red ribbons from the centre of the table, between each place setting, to hang loosely down over the table-cloth. Light the table and the room with red candles to create a soft romantic mood.

EASTER

For a celebration dinner or lunch at Easter, choose colours to create a spring flavour. A bright yellow, green and yellow, or white and yellow cloth with matching or contrasting napkins will set a sunny mood, and napkins can be folded into rabbits' ears for a bit of fun. Bright, flowery china with a predominantly yellow or green pattern will look good against the cloth. Fill a large jug with masses of bright spring flowers — daffodils, jonquils, narcissi, etc. — and place in the middle of the table.

If there are children at the party lay a brightly-wrapped Easter egg and a little fluffy chick or rabbit at each place. Hand-painted eggs also make very good decorations to brighten up the table. At intervals on the table lay little dishes filled with one or other of the following: green Turkish delight, pale green fondant mints, yellow and white sugared almonds, or green grapes dipped in beaten egg-white and castor sugar.

HALLOWE'EN

A Hallowe'en dinner or party is more fun if guests wear fancy dress or masks to create a mood of witchery, black magic and spooks.

Decorate the room with autumn leaves, berries, dried grasses and candles burning in turnip and pumpkin heads with gruesome faces cut from them. Cut out stars and moon shapes in gold, and cats, birds and bats in black, and suspend them from mantle shelves or from the ceiling. Cover the table with a black or dark grey cloth (an old sheet could be dyed) and place in the very centre a large black witch's hat decorated with gold stars and moons and trimmed with autumn leaves. Use black or dark-coloured china and, if possible, dark-handled cutlery, and burn candles in hollowed out pumpkins on the table during the meal.

The food should have an autumnal flavour and should be orange and brown, if possible, to fit the colour scheme. Here are a few ideas:

Devils on horseback — bacon wrapped round prunes stuffed with chicken liver paste, then grilled, served on fingers of fried bread.

32 *Easter: a celebration lunch*

The gold-plated cutlery and beautiful china, with its gold decoration, are ideal for a golden wedding anniversary dinner

Spicy carrot and parsnip soup.

Pumpkin soup.

Goulash made with veal, red peppers and mushrooms.

Lamb stew with carrots.

Pork chops in a barbecue tomato sauce.

Bacon, bean and lentil hot pot.

Stuffed aubergines with a tomato sauce.

Bean and aubergine hot pot.

Baked potatoes with butter or cream cheese.

Roast parsnips.

For dessert, serve baked apples, stuffed with dates, raisins, walnuts, cinnamon and brown sugar with custard and whipped cream, or pears in red wine topped with ice-cream and cream. For a rich but irresistible dessert serve little pots of rich chocolate mousse and call it 'magic mousse' or 'witches' whisk'.

BONFIRE NIGHT

For a bright festive tea party for children on Bonfire Night, choose colours that reflect the bursts from the firework sparks, gold, pink, green, red, blue, etc. Buy or make shiny hats with streamers on the top and place these at each child's place. The table-cloth should be dark to represent the sky at night, and use bright paper napkins. In the middle, have the Bonfire Night Cake (see below).

To decorate the table use brightly-coloured streamers and ribbons trailing from the centre, between each child's place, and hanging over the edge of the table. Place little indoor fireworks around the centre and enjoy these after the food has been eaten, under the strict supervision of an adult. Serve food that can be given special firework names: sausages on sticks are rockets; star-shaped sandwiches or biscuits are star-bursts; slices of

33 *A Hallowe'en party*

34 *A novelty Bonfire Night Cake*

Swiss roll become Catherine wheels, etc. Once the children have filled up on all the goodies inside, they'll be ready to wrap up warmly and watch the fun outside.

The Bonfire Night Cake
Make a Guy Fawkes from a chocolate Swiss roll. Cut one end off for the face, push some small sweets in to create a face and attach the face at right angles to the top of the cake with cocktail sticks. For his arms and legs, push mini Swiss rolls into the sides of the cake. Crumple some red, orange and yellow tissue paper (the flames) and fix to a cake board with glue, leaving a slight hollow in the centre for the Guy. They lay chocolate finger biscuits (the logs) on top of the crumpled paper. Sit the Guy on top of this fire.

Other novelty ideas for the cake are:

A box of fireworks with some of the fireworks popping out.

A giant rocket on a stick.

A large Catherine wheel with sparks flying.

The elegant Christmas table is created by restricting the touches of colour to the central decoration and the individual gifts

9   PLANNING AND SERVING A MEAL

The secret of a successful and attractive meal lies in carefully planning the menu beforehand and co-ordinating it with the table setting. Think of the colours of the food and the colours of the dishes the food will be served and eaten from. A purple-red beetroot soup might not be too appetizing in bright yellow bowls but it would look very attractive in white or very pale green dishes. Although you might enjoy creamy mushroom soup, chicken fricassée and a pale cheesecake on separate occasions, as three courses of the same meal they lack colour, interest and variation in texture.

MENU PLANNING

You should have two main ideas in mind – to create a contrast of colour, texture and flavour in the food and to choose colours and foods that suit the time of year, the occasion, and that do not clash horribly with the china and table setting. Think carefully of garnishes to be used for each dish. They can make all the difference to how appetizing each course looks. So, too, can the selection of vegetables to be served. Roast potatoes, parsnips and artichokes are so similar in colouring that it would be better to choose a green or red vegetable as contrast.

Avoid serving three very rich dishes one after the other and do think of your guests when planning and be aware of possible special requirements. Are any of your guests vegetarians? Does anybody need to avoid certain types of food for health reasons or because of allergies?

Making a work plan
First consider the desired end result, which is that every course should be complete and ready to serve in the correct order. This may mean that a cold dessert can be prepared in advance and stored in the refrigerator or freezer while the rest of the meal is prepared. A hot pudding has to be prepared and ready to go into the oven so that it will cook while earlier courses are being eaten. It is a good general rule to decide what can be fully prepared before-hand and kept cold till needed (such as trifle); or reheated in the microwave or oven when needed (such as a casserole, curry or soup). Allow enough time to lay the table, arrange flowers, fold napkins, etc.

Put wine to chill if necessary and prepare any fiddly garnishes and decorations while there is time before the cooking gets into full swing. Remember that blending in a liquidizer and beating with a rotary whisk are noisy activities and it is better to get these over before guests arrive. Leave enough time to dress and have an apron ready in case there are little jobs still to do that could splash your clothes.

DECORATING FOOD

When presenting any type of food for almost any style of meal it is important to remember that garnishes can make a plate or dish of very ordinary or simple food look really special. Garnishes can range from very simple touches such as a small neat sprig of parsley, a little bunch of mustard and cress leaves, a neat bunch of watercress, a few half slices of cucumber arranged in a fan shape, or a twist of lemon, to quite elaborate garnishes that take a little more time to prepare. When these are placed in the centre of a dish or arranged in strategic positions on or between the food, they can turn a really plain plateful into an attractive, eye-catching and appetizing dish. Several ideas are given below:

Radish roses

Wash the radishes, cut off the stalks and a very thin slice of the root end. Cut thin petals from the root to the stem, taking care not to cut right through; then place the radishes in cold water (preferably iced) until they open out like roses.

35 *Making radish roses*

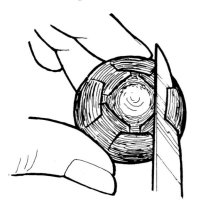

Gherkin fans

Make about six cuts from the top almost to the base of each gherkin, taking care not to cut right through the base. Spread the gherkins out carefully into fan shapes, with the base as a hinge.

Use to garnish cocktail snacks and salads.

36 *Making gherkin fans*

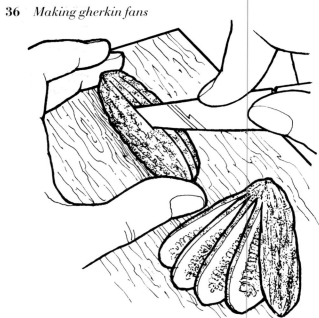

Tomato lilies

Take a clean, firm tomato and, using a sharp knife, halve it by making a series of zigzag cuts. When you have gone right round the tomato, gently pull the halves apart. Alternatively, use a potato peeler to make the zigzag cuts.

Besides being a decorative way of presenting tomatoes as part of a large salad, small cherry tomatoes made into 'lilies' can also garnish hot or cold sliced meats.

37 *Making tomato lilies*

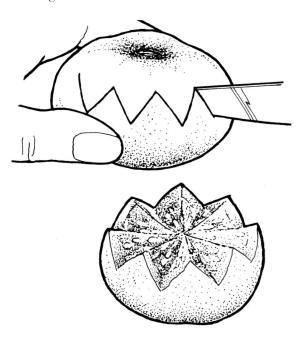

Lemon and orange twists

Take a clean lemon, and slice thinly, discarding the end pieces. Cut through the rind in the middle of each piece up to the centre, then gently twist each half in opposite directions. Use to garnish savoury dishes.

38 *Making lemon twists*

WINES AND OTHER DRINKS

First of all comes the aperitif. This is frequently a sherry or vermouth which you offer your guests as they arrive. It is much better to offer a simple choice than to say 'What would you like to drink?' as this gives them no guideline. Dry sherry is preferable to richer, sweeter sherries. Dry and sweet vermouth are served separately, mixed together, or the former is mixed with gin to make a Martini cocktail. Cocktails are usually based on gin mixed with other aperitifs. A pink gin merely requires the addition of a few drops of Angostura Bitters. Have ready a supply of ice and slices of lemon in case guests prefer gin and tonic.

Sometimes sherry is served with soup and the first wine offered should be a dry white to accompany the hors d'oeuvre and fish courses. A medium dry white or rosé goes well with poultry, veal, or made-up dishes in a white sauce. Red wine is appropriate with red meat or game and with cheese. A sweet, white wine to go with dessert is not obligatory, but it is usual to offer brandy or liqueurs with coffee.

If you have decided not to serve alcohol with the meal, home-made lemonade makes a delicious alternative, especially at lunch-time. Lemons go much further if you steep the squeezed lemon halves in boiling water until this becomes cold. Strain and add to the lemonade. Fizzy drinks, including mineral water, are best served very cold. Pour them at the last moment into tall glasses containing several cubes of ice and serve with decorative straws. Iced black tea or coffee are very refreshing. Add a scoop of vanilla ice cream or a float of cream to the coffee, and a slice of lemon and a sprig of mint, or a few bruised sage leaves, to iced tea.

For a change, to end a dinner party, offer Gaelic

coffee instead of coffee and liqueurs. Warm wine glasses of the short-stemmed goblet shape, pour in a small measure of whisky, add a teaspoon of sugar and stir well. Fill the glasses two-thirds full with strong, hot, black coffee and pour lightly-whipped cream over the back of a teaspoon. The two layers should remain separate.

CARVING

Even today, when many have been converted to vegetarianism, the joint of meat often forms the centre-piece at dinner. It would be a shame, therefore, to have put so much effort into the presentation of the meal, only to have the effect ruined by meat which has not been neatly sliced or by a bird which looks as if it has been pulled apart. Good carving is a skill which can be acquired with just a little time and effort. Once you have built up your confidence, there is no reason why you should not carve at table. It can prove very impressive.

The most important piece of equipment for carving is a long, sharp knife. Armed with this, a two-pronged fork with a handguard and, possibly a second shorter knife, and an ordinary table fork, you should find that a joint of meat will present no difficulty.

Here is a guide showing directions of main cut, rather than the carving position. The fork is used to hold the meat firm against the action of the knife, and the handguard is essential in case the knife slips towards your hand.

Roast rib of beef Place joint upright on a dish, supporting it with the fork, rib side on the left. Cut the first slice down from the outside edge furthest away from you to the rib bone. Remove with the aid of a second fork. Continue carving parallel slices,

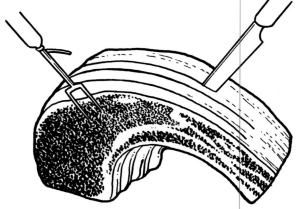

39　*A guide showing the direction of main cut*

40　*Rib of beef*

and if necessary release by sliding the knife at right angles just above and close to the bone.

Round of beef Not so easy as it would appear, unless placed flat on a spiked carving dish. Anchor the joint firmly with the carving fork, then use a very sharp knife, cutting against the support of the fork. Cut a thick slice from the top of the joint leaving it smooth, then carve thin slices.

41 *Round of beef*

Sirloin of beef Place the joint on its side, undercut uppermost. Support with the fork and cut slices through to the bone. Place the joint flat on dish and carve down close to the bone, to release the slices. Reverse process to carve the uppercut of joint.

42 *Sirloin*

Veal top of leg Place the joint on its side, supporting it with the carving fork. Make a V-cut through to the bone and carve slices from each side of the cut. Turn the joint over and carve the other side in the same way.

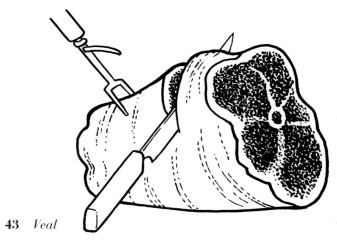

43 *Veal*

Loin of lamb Ask your butcher to chine the joint, that is, saw the backbone through lengthwise. Holding the joint steady with the carving fork, cut down between the bones and serve as chops. A loin can be completely boned by the butcher, stuffed and carved as a round of beef.

Leg of lamb Place the leg so that the thick meaty section is facing you. Insert the fork in the large end of the leg and cut two or three slices, lengthwise, from the thin side of the leg (the side away from you) see fig. 44. Turn the joint to stand on the surface just cut. Insert the fork into the meaty section which should now be on top. Starting at the shank end (the narrow end) cut thin slices down to the large leg bone. With the fork still in place run the knife along the leg bone to release the slices. More slices can now be cut from the underside.

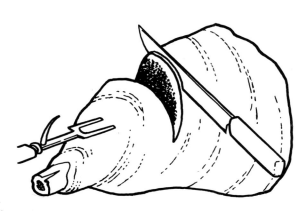

44 *Leg of lamb*

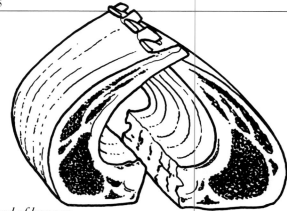

46 *Guard of honour*

Best end of neck Have your butcher prepare and sew together two best ends to make a crown roast, bones outwards (see fig. 45). Fill the centre with stuffing, and carve between the rib bones, dividing the meat into cutlets each with a portion of stuffing. Alternatively, get the butcher to prepare a guard of honour (see fig. 46); the two best ends are placed face to face, bone side inwards, and the trimmed cutlet bones interlaced alternately, to retain the best ends in a standing position.

Shoulder of lamb Raise the joint from the dish with the carving fork and cut slices parallel to the face of the meat. Lay the joint down again and carve the meat on either side of the blade bone and knuckle end.

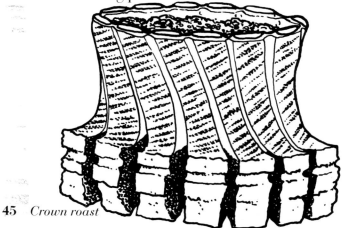

45 *Crown roast*

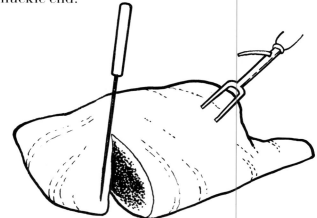

47 *Shoulder of lamb*

Leg of pork Holding the joint down with the carving fork, carry the knife right through the crackling down to the bone, in the same way as for the leg of lamb. Remove some of the crackling if this makes carving easier, and break it up on the plate.

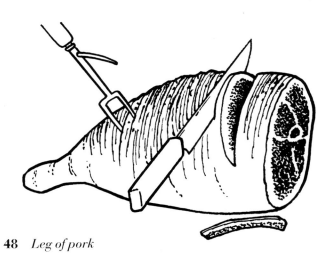

48 *Leg of pork*

Loin of pork Crackling should be scored in diamond shapes so that it divides easily into small portions. Remove some crackling before carving and carve as for loin of lamb.

49 *Roast loin of pork*

Whole ham Place on the dish so that the bone end is at your right. Cut two or three slices from the thin side of the ham, then turn to stand on the surface just cut. Remove a small wedge from the bone end and, with the carving fork steady-

ing the ham, cut thin horizontal slices starting from the wedge. Then run the knife along the leg bone to release the slices. For more slices, turn ham back to first position and cut at right angles to the bone.

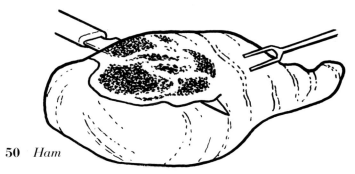

50 *Ham*

Turkey and other poultry Place the bird with legs to the right. Insert the fork just below the breast, being careful not to puncture the breast itself. Slice the thigh and leg from the body. Remove to a separate plate to carve later. Pull the wing from the body as far as possible, work the knife through the joint, twist from the body and remove. Now carve thin slices parallel to the breast bone along the breast meat. Finally, separate the leg from the thigh and cut long thin slices from it with your second shorter knife.

51 *Turkey*

A FORMAL DINNER PARTY

Today's style of entertaining, even on formal occasions, is much more relaxed and easy-going than it used to be. Nevertheless, there are certain accepted rules which need to be followed especially if a large number of people are involved.

1 Lay the table well in advance, leaving time later for cooking. Lay at least two cruet sets if there are more than four people. The same applies to butter dishes and baskets of bread or rolls.

2 Check that the wine has been set to chill or to breathe.

3 If giving the dinner party with someone else, arrange beforehand who will be responsible for what – serving pre-dinner drinks, opening and pouring the wine, serving food and making coffee.

Many people find a three-course dinner more than adequate. Now that the provision of an interesting cheese board is often a feature of the meal, the menu would be too extended if it included more than either soup or hors d'oeuvre, followed by a main course, followed by a dessert, ending with cheese or fruit or possibly both.

Pouring the wine

1 Serve ladies first, ending with the hostess, then the men, ending with the host.

2 As each course finishes serve the wine for the next course.

3 At the end of the meal, offer brandy or liqueurs. If it is a very formal dinner, it may end with port being served from a decanter to 'men only' while the women withdraw to take coffee in another room. Glasses for port should be set only when dessert is served and other wine glasses removed. The decanter of port is passed to the left and never across the table.

Serving the wine

Since wine stains table linen and clothes, take great care not to spill drops while pouring. Wrap a folded napkin round the neck of the bottle and give the bottle a smooth quarter turn as you remove it from the glass after pouring. Be careful not to disturb any sediment in red wine when serving it; but this is a problem which exists only with wines that are old and grand enough to have formed a deposit. If you are serving such a wine it can be decanted before being taken to the table. If the host notices a fragment of cork in a guest's glass, he should unobtrusively remove the glass and if necessary exchange it with his own.

Serving food

Food should be served from the left and used plates removed from the right. No plates should be removed until everyone has finished each course.

If the dinner is being given and served by only one person, it is a good idea to start with an hors d'oeuvre already set on the table, or with soup plates filled before the guests sit down.

Nowadays, it is unlikely that more than one person would be available to help serve at table, or to work behind the scenes in the kitchen. If a maid is employed, she would serve the first course after the party is seated, and then the wine (unless the host or hostess has decided to do this themselves). It is now customary for side plates to be set even on very formal occasions, and unless a maid offers a basket of rolls or bread at the beginning of the meal to each guest in turn, bread baskets should be placed on the table. Guests will then serve themselves with bread and butter throughout the meal.

When the first course is finished, the hors d'oeuvre or soup plates, and any accompaniments,

An appearance of simplicity and elegance is created by leaving the central floral display uncluttered within a ring of candles

should be removed with their service plates by the maid or hostess. If there is a second course – before the main course – it should not have accompanying vegetables which require separate service, as this is much too complicated for a hostess to deal with at home. The plates should be handed round with the course fully served out on each plate. Smooth transition from the first to second courses requires either the hostess to prepare the plates and the maid to pass them round, or if there is a helper in the kitchen she can prepare the plates and the hostess will pass them. Where there is no helper at all, the host will probably assist the hostess both to clear and serve, and take the opportunity of getting up from the table to refill wine glasses or pour the second wine. Quite often the second course is omitted, and the main course served after the hors d'oeuvre or soup.

There are two ways to deal with the service of a hot main course. Either the hostess or a helper serves out portions complete with vegetables for each guest in the kitchen, and these are carried round; or plates with the main course are put in front of the guests, and vegetable dishes and sauce-boats are placed on the table to be passed round.

Remember it is very important to speed up service before food becomes cold, as guests are reluctant to begin eating before everyone has been served, even if invited to do so. Service is very slow if a helper or maid carries round vegetable dishes offering them to each guest, so this should be avoided. It is not usual, at formal dinners, to offer second helpings. If a second wine is served at the beginning of the main course it should be poured either by the host or hostess, or by the maid. Do not remove glasses which have already been used; some people may prefer to continue with white wine. When the main course is finished, remove the plates, dishes and cruet sets.

Desserts may be served either from the kitchen or the serving dish may be set on the table. This is best if the dessert is a beautifully decorated gâteau or other creation. Individual dessert dishes should be brought in with any necessary items such as cream jugs, sugar bowls. These are all removed afterwards. The cheese board or tray is then brought in and circulated. Guests should use their side plates or be given a fresh small plate.

When port is not served, the coffee tray may be brought to the table after the cheeseboard has been cleared and fresh fruit has been offered. When there is no fresh fruit, delicate chocolate mints or petits fours are often handed out with coffee. The host or hostess usually pours the coffee, although it may be handed round quite informally by the guests themselves. Fresh coffee should be available if the 'gentlemen' are to 'join the ladies' after the port.

10   CARING FOR TABLEWARE

When you have spent both time and money choosing tableware that is suited to your lifestyle, it is important that you know how to keep these things looking as good as new. This chapter is full of useful tips for cleaning, storing and removing stains from all your tableware.

TABLE SURFACES AND CHAIRS

Wood
With the exception of whitewood, all wooden furniture has been given a final surface treatment by the manufacturer. That is why it is important to know what the material is when you buy and, if possible, obtain advice on how to care for it. If the original finish is to keep its looks, it needs a certain amount of regular attention.

Day-by-day care should be kept to dusting; cleaning and/or polishing should be done weekly. This gives a better effect than daily polishing. Some surfaces do not need polishing. It is important to remove dirt thoroughly (see below) to prevent a layer of dirt, mixed with polish, from building up. Always use heat-proof mats to prevent the surface from being marked.

Wax polish Furniture that has been wax-polished really does need elbow grease to bring it up. A good furniture wax can be used occasionally, but sparingly, because the solvent in the polish softens the basic wax leaving a smeary surface. So always use the minimum and buff well. Teak and 'oiled' woods need a few drops of teak oil every three or four months.

French polish The high gloss of a french polish should last for years if handled carefully. Polish occasionally with a little beeswax-based furniture cream and remove any build-up of wax with a mixture of one part vinegar to eight parts water. Remove sticky marks with a little warm soapy water, dry thoroughly afterwards. Heat marks should disappear if rubbed with linseed oil or olive oil and cigarette ash or cigar ash (these mild abrasives could be added to the oil without harm). Old or worn french polish is best removed and a new surface applied professionally although DIY kits are available.

Stain removal from wood surfaces
Treat all stains as soon as possible. White heat marks that have not penetrated too deeply should be gently rubbed with a soft cloth dipped in camphorated oil. Treat a small part at a time and wipe away any surplus oil. Wax and polish in the normal way.

Persistent marks can be camouflaged by a special wood dye (following the manufacturer's instructions); burns that have penetrated the surface may mean stripping and re-polishing. A deep burn that has destroyed the wood can only be masked by staining and polishing.

Hot grease is ideally removed at once with soft paper. If set, lift off with a blunt knife. Use the same method for melted candle wax. Polish well.

There are various methods of removing bad water marks such as glass rings. One method is to soak very fine steel wool in furniture cream and polish hard over the mark. This may be successful, but if not try rubbing with linseed oil or olive oil and a little cigarette or cigar ash, as these are mild abrasives. Afterwards polish the mark very hard with a slightly tinted furniture cream or dye. When the mark has nearly disappeared, wax and polish in the usual way. Ordinary iodine is useful to touch up scratches on dark woods. Make a trial application first on a small area and if the result is too dark dilute it with alcohol. For lighter woods, rub the scratch with a fresh shelled and halved Brazil nut.

Plastic finishes

Modern clear 'plastic' finishes protect furniture well against dust, grease and grime. A gloss finish is best maintained with the occasional use of a cleaning and polishing liquid; a matt finish should be wiped lightly with a moist chamois leather. Too much polishing on matt surfaces will destroy the matt effect, causing an ugly 'bloom'. Once you begin using polish you may find you need to do it regularly.

Laminates

Laminates require nothing beyond a wipe with a damp cloth. If you do use a little household cleaner be sure to rinse all traces away with a clean damp cloth. Drying with a soft cloth prevents smearing.

Eggshell paint

This should be washed over with warm water and a mild detergent. A small amount of white furniture cream used occasionally will improve the surface.

Bamboo

To clean bamboo wipe with a damp cloth and pat dry with a soft absorbent cloth. If badly soiled, add a tablespoon of common salt to every 500 ml (1 pint) of water and apply with a soft brush. Wipe dry with a soft cloth, then rub the surface with a piece of velvet soaked in linseed oil. Leave for an hour or so, then polish with a soft cloth.

Canework and rush

Canework should be vacuum-dusted using a rubber upholstery nozzle. Old and grubby cane can be cleaned using a soft brush and a *minimum* of warm, slightly soapy water. Do small sections at a time; wipe away any soap traces with a clean damp cloth and pat dry with a colourfast towel. Rush seating should be similarly vacuumed. Avoid using water unless advised otherwise when purchasing.

Most modern bamboo, cane and rushwork is 'sealed' during manufacturing stages with chemical agents. Be extra careful to make a permanent note of the furniture maker's cleaning instructions.

Marble

Marble can be cleaned by lightly scouring with powdered borax and then washing with plain warm water. When this treatment is not effective a solution of oxalic acid can be applied. Proprietary cleaners are also available.

Glass and mirror surfaces

Glass table tops if very dirty should first be rubbed with damp crumpled newspaper. Then use a damp chamois leather, polishing after with a dry one. You may also use a special window cleaning preparation or general household cleaner, but do watch for overpowering perfumes. Put on with absorbent paper or cloth and polish off with a clean rag.

Mirrored surfaces may be cleaned with the same proprietary cleaners as glass. Alternatively use a soft cloth with methylated spirit.

Steel and chrome

Tubular steel is cleaned with a modern 'sparkle' polish and chrome with a proprietary chrome cleaner, following the maker's instructions.

Upholstery

Upholstery should be brushed or vacuumed regularly and shampooed occasionally with a branded cleaner. Take care not to overwet the fabric and aid drying by opening windows or switching on a fan heater. Avoid spraying polish on to chair upholstery by applying to wood parts with a cloth. Grease marks respond to a grease solvent or to a hot iron and blotting paper. Place the paper over the mark and iron gently. (This technique may also be used with carpets.)

Vinyl and plastic materials should be regularly wiped with a damp, soapy cloth. Wipe away any soap traces with a clean damp cloth and buff away moisture drops with a soft rag.

The beauty of real leather seat covers can be preserved by the same treatment. Treat occasionally with light application of 'hide-food' — branded preparations are available.

TABLE-CLOTHS AND NAPKINS

Care of table linens will depend on the materials from which they are made. By and large, synthetics require less attention than most pure cottons and linens, or mixtures of natural and man-made fibres. But the beauty of starched cloths and napkins is often well worth the effort involved in laundering and ironing them.

Synthetic fabrics should be washed in accordance with maker's directions but as a general rule they may be either machine-washed on the appropriate programme or hand-washed in warm water. Hand-washed articles may be pre-soaked but should not be wrung out, simply drip-dried. Usually ironing is not necessary, although some fibres can be lightly pressed with a warm iron if liked. Synthetic fabrics should not be starched.

Natural fibres such as cotton and linen may be machine-washed (delicate hand woven linens, embroidery or lace-worked articles should be placed inside an old pillow case); but many people prefer to hand-wash. Pre-wash soaking in tepid water for about half an hour will loosen small particles of grime and any marks or stains. Whites are washed in very hot water and boiled every few washes to retain whiteness. Coloured linens should be tested for colour fastness by ironing between pieces of cotton. Fast colours can then be washed in cooler water. Cotton organdie is similarly treated. All natural fibres, except seersuckers and similar 'bubble' materials, may be starched (see below).

Thorough rinsing in clean water will help to keep your table linen gleaming and fresh. Greying linens may be brightened up with good old-fashioned blueing agents. These come in powder or liquid form, and it is essential to dissolve them thoroughly or spotting will occur. Articles should be loosely immersed and evenly wetted in the solution. If a cloth is over-blued a further rinse in warm water with a splash of white vinegar will adjust the tint.

There is now a range of stain and dye removing agents readily available. Each stain remover is clearly marked with the type of stain for which it is effective, such as ink, blood, wine, etc. There is also a stain remover to remove loose dye from white material. All you have to do is to soak the fabric in water for a couple of hours.

This may be helpful for established tea-stains or other persistent food stains in table linen.

Starching

Only starched napkins can be folded into ornamental shapes that stay put. With powder starches that dissolve in water, table linens are starched wet immediately following washing/rinsing. If necessary fold each item neatly and dip one at a time. Hang out to dry keeping as flat as possible. Aerosol starches should be evenly sprayed on to damp linen. Starching is easier to iron while still damp. If it does over-dry, damp-down by sprinkling with water, folding and rolling into a small parcel. Leave for about an hour. Always iron from the centre out, gently pulling the napkins and cloths into shape: they should have good square corners and really straight edges.

Ironing and folding table linens

All table linen, especially if starched, needs to be correctly folded: then it will store without creasing and those odd diamond shaped folds which seem to appear by magic will be an irritation of the past.

Table mats Iron starched table mats flat on both sides, teasing out with your fingers fringed edges that have become tangled. They may also need some persuasive stretching to become completely square again.

Embroidery on cloths and napkins should be pressed face down onto a soft cloth or towel to restore its beauty. The plain parts are first ironed and folded as above.

Lace Cotton lace should be ironed from the centre out while being gently pulled into shape. Delicate lace should be protected between sheets of tissue paper.

CHINA

Take care when washing-up to use warm soapy water with the detergent liquid well dissolved. Too hot water or neat detergent poured onto the china will in time spoil both colour and glaze. Rinse in clean warm water and drain, allow to drip dry and polish with a soft cloth, or wipe dry. Most china can be placed in a dish washer, but, where the china is very valuable, it is wiser to wash it by hand. This rule certainly applies to china decorated with gold leaf or other precious metal decoration.

Do not put plates into a hot oven or under the grill to warm unless sold as oven-proof.

Stains

Silver stains from cutlery can easily be removed from china by a silver polish. Do not use harsh abrasives as they will remove the glaze. A small amount of salt on a dish cloth will shift tea stains. Alternatively soak in detergent solution.

Fill a badly stained teapot with detergent suds to which has been added a good teaspoon of salt. Allow to stand for one hour, then rinse out thoroughly.

Storing best china

In spite of the fact that cups look very nice on hooks,

it is not a good way of storing your best ones, since there is too much weight on delicate handles. If you store valuable plates in piles, protect them from scratching by interleaving with soft tissue or cloth. Allow plenty of space for storing your best china rather than pile it into a small cupboard where it can easily be damaged.

CUTLERY

The best method of caring for all cutlery, whatever it is made from, is to wash and dry immediately after use. In this way all food residues are removed before staining can occur. No cutlery is totally stain-resistant, so do not leave it unwashed, wet or 'in soak' overnight – even in a dish washer. First rinse under cold running water to remove any traces of salt; salt plus hot water can cause staining and pitting. Next wash in clean, warm, soapy water, rinse and dry thoroughly. Use soft dish pads or cloths and tea towels, and never add bleach to the water. Handle each piece separately; cutlery cluttered in a bowl may get scratched. When drying, knife blades (nowadays usually made from stainless steel) should not be wiped with an up-and-down movement, but in one direction only from neck to point until all the moisture is removed. This method is best for spoons and forks too.

Stainless steel cutlery While stainless steel requires very little special attention, the above routine should still be followed. Any stains that do occur are usually due to an accidental application of silver cleaning material or to prolonged contact with acids and minerals – salt, vinegar or even those naturally present in tap water. Steel wool fragments can cause rust marks if carelessly left in contact as can corrosion pitting, although this is only likely to occur in cheap imported pieces. Very hard water can deposit a chalky film and very hot fat or meat juices (and of course direct heat if cutlery is left on a hot plate) can cause stubborn rainbow stains. Most stains that resist ordinary rubbing with a soapy cloth can be corrected with Goddard's stainless steel care.

Horn and wood handles Cutlery with handles of horn or natural polished wood should not be machine washed, nor even placed bodily into water. Simply hold each piece by the handle and wash only the metal parts. As the handles may become damp, dry each thoroughly as soon as possible. Plastic-finished woods do not need polish, but if plunged in water frequently they become grey and dull.

China and stoneware These handles should be washed as china. Certain types of plastic handles which look like China should not be subjected to the heat of dish washers so note manufacturer's instructions.

Silver and silver plate including EPNS (electro-plated nickel silver) should be washed and dried as above and never in a dish washer. Silver is a comparatively soft metal and no matter what care is taken it is inevitable that small scratches will appear on the polished surface. This results in a less brilliant, but no less attractive appearance. Tarnishing is easily removed by a good silver polish. 'Long term' polishes are probably the best as they do provide a high degree of protection against subsequent tarnishing. A silver dip is useful for keeping fork prongs and teaspoons immaculate. Silver cleaners should never be brought into contact with stainless steel knife blades because it can damage them.

Pewter This is a real easy-care metal, but if tarnished through non-use, the lustre can be restored with silver polish. Otherwise, treat as stainless steel.

The dramatic simplicity of the black and white china and cutlery is heightened by the intense colours of the anemones

Bronze and vermeil Wash these, and gilded stainless steel cutlery, as silver. They should not tarnish.

Storing cutlery
The ideal way to store cutlery is in a canteen. These can be purchased separately from leading stores or can be made by the home handyman. Choose between the open box or cabinet drawer type, free-standing or on legs. A plain felt lining and a sectioned insert for convenient stacking will keep cutlery well protected and tidy.

Alternatively use a carry box divided into sections and similarly lined. A piece of loose felt laid over the cutlery will keep dust and damp away. Felts should be softly brushed to keep them clean.

GLASSWARE
Fine glass, particularly valuable crystal, should be washed by hand and not in a dish washer. Use a plastic bowl or a rubber mat in the sink and warm, not hot, soapy water with a soft cloth or sponge. Pressed or engraved patterns can be cleaned with a soft brush. Glasses used for milk or alcoholic beverages should be pre-rinsed in cold water. Wash one glass at a time to prevent chipping and rinse in plain warm water. Some people like to add a splash of vinegar to the rinsing water to remove all soap or detergent traces. Drain on a rubber mat or plastic-coated drainer or on a folded towel. When clearing up after a party, take a tip from the publicans and cover trays with cloths or kitchen paper, leaving glasses to drain.

Stain removal
Obstinate marks on glass are dissolved by soaking the glass for twenty-four hours in a strong solution of household detergent and water or rubbing very carefully with a cleaning powder. For lime deposits use tea leaves soaked in vinegar. If the problem is excessive caking on the inside of a bottle or decanter the addition of a little silver sand will be helpful. Swirl round vigorously before pouring it out.

Stuck glasses and stoppers
When glasses stick together do not attempt to pry them apart. Pour cold water on the inner glass and hold the outer one in warm water. Stoppers which stick can eventually be removed from decanters by rubbing a little cooking oil around the joint and leaving in a warm place. But a certain amount of patience may be needed.

Storage
Glasses not in regular use can be packed away safely in cardboard boxes. Wrap glasses individually in tissue paper or newspaper and lay side by side in alternate rows, rims to bases, with layers separated by several sheets of paper. Alternatively use strong scissors and make proper cardboard box dividers or save the ones used in cases of wine for this purpose. They fold flat when not required. Glasses that have been stored should always be washed before use. At first glance they may look clean, but are probably dusty or at best, less than sparkling.

MENU DESIGNS

MENU

Stilton and watercress pâté

Beef olives
Duchess Potato nests with peas
Glazed carrots

Caramelized oranges

Coffee

Wine: Rosé

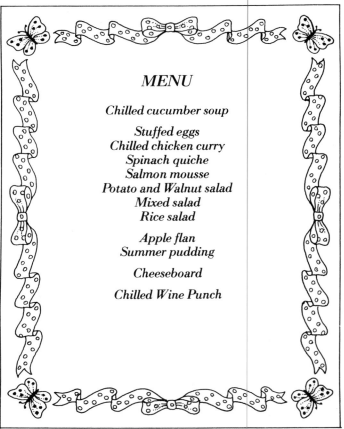

MENU

Chilled cucumber soup

Stuffed eggs
Chilled chicken curry
Spinach quiche
Salmon mousse
Potato and Walnut salad
Mixed salad
Rice salad

Apple flan
Summer pudding

Cheeseboard

Chilled Wine Punch

52   *A birthday dinner party for six people*

53   *A christening buffet lunch for twenty people*

INDEX

Page numbers in *italics* refer to diagrams and illustrations

ACKNOWLEDGMENTS

The author and publishers would like to thank the
following for supplying photographs:
Anthony Blake Photo Library, page 60; The China
and Glass Retailers Association, photograph
supplied by Josephine Hawkins (Chief Executive),
page 57; Crown Paints, page 36; Duplikat (Duni
Ltd), page 24; Tim Hill, front jacket and page 76;
Interior Selection, back jacket and page 53; Michael
Boys Syndication, page 69; Nairn Kingfisher Ltd,
from the Kingfisher Collection, page 41; Rosenthal
China (London) Ltd, pages 44 and 49; Royal
Worcester Spode Ltd, page 16; A Sanderson & Sons
Ltd, pages 8 and 37.